ENCOURAGING
Women

Christian women write on living out your faith

ENCOURAGING
Women

Christian women write on living out your faith

CWR, Waverley Abbey House, Waverley Lane, Farnham, Surrey GU9 8EP

National Distributors
UK (and countries not listed below) CWR, PO Box 230, Farnham, Surrey GU9 8XG
Tel: 01252 784710 Outside UK (44) 1252 784710
AUSTRALIA: CMC Australasia, PO Box 519, Belmont,Victoria 3216
Tel: (03) 5241 3288
CANADA: CMC Distribution Ltd., PO Box 7000, Niagara on the Lake, Ontario
LoS 1Jo Tel: 1 800 325 1297
HONG KONG: Cross Communications Ltd, Flat B, 11/F, KO's House, 577
Nathan Road, Kowloon Tel: 852 2780 1188/2384 0880
INDIA: Full Gospel Literature Stores, 254 Kilpauk Garden Road, Chennai
600010 Tel: (44) 644 3073
KENYA: Keswick Bookshop, PO Box 10242, Nairobi Tel: (02) 331692/226047
MALAYSIA: Salvation Book Centre (M), 23 Jalan SS2/64, Sea Park, 47300
Petaling Jaya, Selangor Tel: (3) 7766411
NEW ZEALAND: CMC New Zealand Ltd., Private Bag, 17910 Green Lane,
Auckland Toll free: 0800 333639
NIGERIA: FBFM, (Every Day with Jesus), Prince's Court, 37 Ahmed Onibudo
Street, PO Box 70952, Victoria Island Tel: 01 2617721, 616832, 4700218
PHILIPPINES: Praise Incorporated, 145 Panay Avenue, Cor Sgt Esguerra St,
Quezon City Tel: 632 920 5291
REPUBLIC OF IRELAND: Scripture Union, 40 Talbot Street, Dublin 1
Tel: (01) 8363764
SINGAPORE: Campus Crusade Asia Ltd., 315 Outram Road, 06–08 Tan Boon
Liat Building, Singapore 169074 Tel: (65) 222 3640
SOUTH AFRICA: Struik Christian Books (Pty Ltd), PO Box 193, Maitland 7405,
Cape Town Tel: (021) 551 5900
SRI LANKA: Christombu Investments, 27 Hospital Street, Colombo 1
Tel: (1) 433142/328909
USA: CMC Distribution, PO Box 644, Lewiston, New York 14092-0644
Tel: 1 800 325 1297

ENCOURAGING WOMEN
Copyright © 1999 CWR and Woman Alive except "Work and God's Purpose"
extracted from *Split Image*, copyright © 1998 Anne Atkins. Reproduced by
permission of Hodder and Stoughton Ltd.

Front cover photograph: The Stock Market
Design and Typesetting: CWR Production and *Start*.
Printed in Great Britain by Clifford Frost Ltd.

ISBN 1 85345 135 5

All rights reserved, including serialisation and translation. No part of this
publication may be reproduced, stored in a retrieval system, or transmitted, in
any form or by any means, electronic, mechanical, photocopying, recording or
otherwise, without the prior permission in writing of CWR or *Woman Alive*.

Unless otherwise indicated, all Scripture references are from the Holy Bible:
New International Version (NIV). Copyright © 1973, 1978, 1984 by the
International Bible Society.

Woman Alive, 96 Dominion Road, Worthing, West Sussex BN14 8JP

Contents

Introduction

I remember the autumn of 1996 well. It was a time of personal blessing and of personal upset. At work, *Woman Alive*, which I had been editing for two years, was finally gaining ground and being accepted as the leading monthly magazine for Christian women. At home my husband had just confirmed that he wished our year-long separation to become permanent.

So it was with mixed feelings that I made my first trip to Crusade for World Revival, based at Waverley Abbey House, for a special women's weekend led by Selwyn Hughes on "Relationships". Childcare arrangements and the thought of driving somewhere totally unknown on a Friday night, meant that I decided to miss the initial session and join the group at Waverley on Saturday morning instead. As I drove along the Sussex country lanes through the early morning mist I felt less than enthusiastic about a weekend away – especially one discussing the delicate subject of relationships. But at the back of my mind I knew God wanted me at Waverley that weekend.

The teaching was excellent and, despite the "sensitive" subject matter, I gained a tremendous insight into all aspects of relationships. My fellow guests were great; we shared, prayed and laughed together. But God had something else in mind besides personal refreshment; it was during this weekend that I first met Jeannette Barwick, coordinator of CWR's women's ministry, and we discussed the possibility of putting on an event to draw women together for a time of celebration and teaching. "How wonderful it would be," we said, "if we could somehow get women of all ages and denominations together for an afternoon or evening of celebration." We prayed, "Lord, if You are in this idea then let it grow according to Your will."

Three years on, that idea has indeed grown into something neither Jeannette or myself could have envisaged back in 1996. Thousands of women have now attended *Alive for God* events at major towns and cities around the UK. Women have "voted with their feet" and come out in force! Yes, they *do* feel the need to come together for fellowship and encouragement; and yes, they *do* want to take time out to hear leading Christian women speakers whom they might not otherwise get to hear in their home churches.

We have received many letters of encouragement from women who have attended meetings. One lady in Manchester described how *Alive for God* had "relit a flame in hearts that were jaded with religion"; another in Brighton wrote saying how "encouraging it was to see hundreds of women of all ages worshipping together".

What is especially exciting about all this, is that *Alive for God* is just a part of an overall increase in events for women. I recently heard from a lady who felt it was high time that men stopped relegating women to secondary roles within the church. She wrote with determination about how we need to discover what is fact, not just tradition or fear, in relation to women's roles. She added: "There do seem to be a few more women's conferences and perhaps this was 'God's way in'."

Well, that certainly seems to be our experience here at *Woman Alive* and CWR. We are sure that God is moving women on – building them up in their faith, equipping them to do His work. "God's way in" seems to be less about fighting the system, and more about offering ourselves as women, united in our service for Him – and letting Him open the doors.

I am thrilled to be able to introduce this book, which includes contributions from all the main speakers on the *Alive for God* tour. My prayer is that God will use the testimonies and Bible teaching that they share as a source of inspiration – that *Encouraging Women* will be a tool in helping women to discover God's will for their lives and, most importantly, to remind all its readers of His unfailing love for them as individuals.

Liz Proctor

Editor, *Woman Alive*

February 1999

CHAPTER ONE

HOPE – THE ANCHOR OF THE SOUL

Irene Addison

—— ⬥ ——

Biography

Born in a small town in the highlands of Scotland, Irene Addison heard the Gospel for the first time at the age of seventeen. A dynamic encounter with Jesus Christ two years later brought radical change to her life and circumstances and launched her into a life of service for God.

She has two daughters and now lives in Aberdeen, Scotland. Together with her husband, she pastors a lively and active Church and teaches in its Bible School. Irene also co-edits the publication *Voice of the Preacher.*

Today her preaching and tape ministry extends to four continents. She ministers sound biblical truth with a strong prophetic edge. Her teaching has a clarity and freshness which brings revelation and understanding to everyone who has a hunger to hear from God.

Her heart is to see others raised up to live without compromise, loving God, serving Him wholeheartedly and loving it!

What a great day it was when I sat my driving test for the fourth time. My previous three attempts had been fraught with anxiety and a fearful kind of hope, that if nothing unforeseen happened, if everyone else drove the way they should, if I somehow managed to get through the dreaded reversing round a corner, if I was able to answer all my highway code questions right – then maybe, just maybe, I would pass. I hoped so anyway!

I had taken extra lessons, studied my highway code every moment of the day. I had prayed, asking God's help and hoped that on the day of my test He would somehow give me what I needed to enable me to pass.

I expect you are asking, "Well did you pass, or didn't you?!" The answer is "Yes! I did," but there was something my examiner said, which prepared me for the test in a way that nothing else had. He said this, "Before you drive off, Mrs Addison, I want you to know that I am not looking for any reason to fail you – I want you to pass your test today!"

At that moment something happened in the realm of my mind. Subconsciously I had been wrongly thinking that my examiner was looking for something to disqualify me when the exact opposite was the truth. It was as if an explosion of truth went off on the inside of me and suddenly I had hope of a different kind. It was the kind of hope which enabled me to sit that fourth driving test with the confidence that I would never have to sit it again.

It was after this experience that I began to allow God to do a deep work in my heart concerning hope. As I meditated on it, I began to understand that there are two different kinds of hope and the two are completely incompatible with one another.

Hopeful or fearful

On the one hand there is the hope that is rooted in fear and apprehension. We all know it well – "I hope I pass my exams, I hope everything turns out OK, I hope I'll have enough money to pay that bill, I hope I never have to go to hospital, I hope I'll pass my driving test." Well, every time I sat my driving test I was definitely hoping I would pass, but lurking right at the root of that hope was the fear I would fail.

I want to challenge you to check your heart out right now and you may find that, without realising it, you have always viewed your Heavenly Father in the same way as I viewed my driving examiner. Subconsciously you see God as one who is looking for your faults, one who is more conscious of your weaknesses than your strengths. Intellectually you believe God is a good God, but underlying that belief is the fear that perhaps He has some disappointment or failure or disaster in store for you – but you hope not! The truth is, God has no defeat or failure planned for you. God wants you to have the very best out of life. That is why He sent His Son Jesus to die for you. It was to redeem you, or buy you back, out of a life of hopelessness and fear and despair: "For I know the thoughts and plans that I have for you, says the Lord, thoughts and plans for welfare and peace and not for evil, to give you *hope* in your final outcome" (Jer. 29:11, Amp. Bible).

Hope that is based on fear is not the God-kind of hope. As a teenager I would often find myself saying, "I hope my father doesn't find out!" Sounds familiar doesn't it? But I discovered that fear has a habit of producing the very thing it is afraid of! That is because fear is not just a feeling, but a spirit which God has not given us.

When the apostle Paul wrote to Timothy, who was a young minister of God in the making, he encouraged him to stir up the gift of God in him saying, "God has not given us a *spirit of fear,* but of power and of love and of a sound mind" (2 Tim. 1:7, NKJ). Paul was writing to Timothy in the midst of a very difficult situation because he knew from his own experience that the spirit of fear was trying to intimidate Timothy as he sought to serve God.

Job also discovered that what he was experiencing in life was the product of what he greatly feared: "For the thing which I greatly fear comes upon me and that of which I am afraid befalls me" (Job 3:25, Amp. Bible).

It is true to say that whatever you are afraid of heads straight for you, whether it is spiders, dogs, sickness or anything else. Fear is like a magnet and that is why you need to get rid of it. Perfect love is the only thing that has the power to deal with fear. The Amplified Bible puts it this way: "There is no fear in love [dread does not exist], but full-grown (complete, perfect) love turns fear out of doors and expels every trace of terror!" (1 John 4:18).

When you are filled with the love of God, when you realise how much He loves you, fear is displaced and hope rises up on the inside – the God-kind of hope! This is so different from what many of us have experienced in life.

Many of us have put our hope in people at different times and been hurt or betrayed. Children have put their hope in parents who have failed them and they have become bitter and disappointed. Such experiences can make it difficult for us to trust anyone, with the result that we never again raise our hopes for fear of further disappointments. Instead we settle for superficial relationships which seem safe but lack any lasting commitment and produce the very thing we fear.

The truth is that when you allow Jesus to expel every trace of fear you develop the confidence to express genuine love knowing that God is the defence of your life.

Money is not the answer

Many people put their hope in their salary, their pension plan or in some inheritance which may be heading their way, but is this really the way God intends for us to live?

In 1 Timothy 6:17 (Amp. Bible) Paul says this: "As for the rich in this world, charge them not to be proud and arrogant and contemptuous of others, nor to set their hopes on uncertain riches!"

We live in an age when there is a great tendency to think that money is the answer to everything. Rich people will tell you that this is not the case. The uncertainty of riches is that they can be here today and gone tomorrow. One generation may work hard to build a great financial resource and the next generation may squander it. Riches can never buy happiness or health or fulfillment. Many rich people never discover who their real friends are until their money is gone!

Now, of course, there is nothing wrong with being rich, but the instruction is not to put our hope in riches but in God Himself, "Who richly and ceaselessly provides us with everything for our enjoyment" (1 Tim. 6:17, Amp. Bible). When you put your hope in God, rather than riches, your whole attitude to life changes.

What was the apostle Paul's instruction concerning wealthy people? It was this: "Charge them to do good, to be rich in good works, to be liberal and generous of heart, ready to share with others" (1 Tim. 6:18, Amp. Bible).

This, of course, is a principle of life which applies to everyone. God wants to take each one of us out of a "give me" mentality, out of a need-centred way of thinking and into a place where we can actually meet the needs of others. In other words, God wants to change mission-fields into missionaries! Paul went on to say, "In this way you will be laying up for yourself the riches that endure forever as a good foundation for the future, so that you may grasp that which is life indeed" (1 Tim. 6:19, Amp. Bible).

You see, life does not consist of the abundance of things a man possesses. The only way you can lay a good foundation for the future is by setting your hope, not on uncertain riches, but on God Himself! This is the God-kind of hope that I am talking about.

Hope originates with God

The God-kind of hope simply means: *To anticipate with confident expectation.*

This is the kind of hope God put in your heart before you were ever born. King David understood this when he said: "You are He Who took me out of the womb; You made me hope and trust when I was on my mother's breasts" (Ps. 22:9, Amp. Bible).

It is a wonderful thing to watch a new-born baby. Whenever he is picked up, he looks for one thing – nourishment! It doesn't matter if that baby is picked up by male or female, he will snuggle in, mouth open, searching for a breast or bottle to feed from.   That baby's hope is in God. His hope has been in God from conception. If that tiny specimen of humanity could speak, he would say, "Where is the food, then? I know it must be here somewhere because God has been nourishing me and

11

feeding me for nine months already. He has been knitting me together in my mother's womb. I know God's provision is here somewhere!" That baby is anticipating with confident expectation that God's continued provision is there for him.

So you see the God-kind of hope was in you from birth. God put it there. Hope of this kind, however, has to be sustained, because where there are no godly parents to nurture that hope and dependence on God, hope dies and is replaced with the world's alternative that is based on fear. That child will begin to put hope in people, hope in uncertain riches, hope in achievement, hope in everything but God Himself.

Hope is for a lifetime

Abraham was a man whose hope was in God even in old age. When all human reason for hope was gone, Abraham kept hoping in faith. He did not weaken in faith when he looked at a seemingly hopeless situation. No doubt or unbelief made him waver or doubtingly question concerning the promise of God. He was fully satisfied within himself that God was able and mighty to keep the promises He had made to him (Rom. 4:18–21).

Abraham did not allow himself to brood on impossibility but kept meditating on the promise of God. He kept praising and thanking God for the fulfillment of His promises and, as a result, he grew strong and was empowered by faith. Because of this, hope did not diminish, it increased and Abraham's faith was credited to him as righteousness.

Get anchored in hope

You too can lay hold of the promises of God for your life. As you give praise and glory to God, as you put your hope in God Himself you will begin to see His promises fulfilled in your life. You will lay hold of the good future God has for you – not the future the devil would like to give you: "I know the thoughts and plans that I have for you, says the Lord, thoughts and plans for welfare and peace and not for evil, to give you hope in your final outcome" (Jer. 29:11, Amp. Bible). That means you don't have to live a moment longer in the fear of what might or might not happen.

God has only good plans for your life. Instead of a pension-plan, He has a "hope-plan" prepared for you. The book of Hebrews tells us that, through Jesus Christ, we have this hope, the God-kind of hope as an anchor for the soul (6:19). That is a tremendous hope to have! Hope of this kind acts as an anchor for the soul. The soul is your mind (what you think), your will (what you want) and your emotions (what you feel).

It is not difficult to understand then why so many people are unstable mentally, physically and emotionally. The problem is that their soul is not anchored in hope. They are not conforming to God in purpose, thought and action, for that is what righteousness is. They are so obsessed with their own thoughts and opinions, so concerned with how they feel, so taken up with their own desires that they become governed by their feelings rather than by faith. What is the problem? Their main concern is not what God thinks, what God wants or how God feels, but what they think, want and feel.

Hope is the only thing that can anchor your soul. When your purpose is God's purpose, your thoughts are God's thoughts and your lifestyle conforming to God, then God Himself becomes the stabilising factor in your life. Your soul must be anchored in hope in order for you to enjoy a Spirit-led, stress-free life.

Be ruled by the Spirit

Having God's interests at heart is one of the main keys to being led and ruled by the Spirit. King David learned how to be ruled by the Spirit of God rather than his soul. There were times when he would speak to his soul: "Why are you downcast, O my soul?" he asked himself (Ps. 42:11). Everyone experiences such feelings. Maybe someone has let you down, leaving you with a feeling of disappointment. Perhaps you have failed in some area of life and you feel discontented or frustrated. There are so many feelings we can experience at different times, but if we choose to submit to our feelings there will always be something the devil can use to keep us downtrodden and defeated.

King David was facing a serious situation:"O my God, my life is cast down upon me [and I find the burden more than I can bear]" (Ps. 42:6, Amp. Bible). I'm sure almost everyone has felt like this at some point in life and can identify with how David was feeling. What did he do in the face of such overwhelming emotions?

He began to take authority over his soul. He began to demand a reason for his own downheartedness: "Why are you downcast, O my soul? Put your hope in God!" In other words, he began to command his soul, "Stop your nonsense, O my soul. What right do you have to be downcast? Now submit to the Holy Spirit! Hope in God! Hope in God and wait expectantly for Him. No storm lasts forever, soul. Now let's give glory to God in this situation."

David did not dwell on negative feelings or allow them to control him. He began to express his hope in God: "Yet the Lord will command His loving-kindness in the daytime, and in the night His song shall be with me, a prayer to the God of my life" (Ps. 42:8, Amp. Bible).

That is why it is so important when you go to bed at night to have the song of the Lord in your heart. Don't think about your problems, don't think about your bills, don't harbour any offence against anyone in your heart, don't think about that person who has upset you. Hope in God and wait expectantly for Him! Your thoughts and feelings must never be allowed to rule your life. Feelings are fickle but God never changes. You must teach your soul how to submit to the rule of the Holy Spirit.

I discovered for myself that when things were tough I had a choice. I could allow that situation to be a stumbling block or make it a stepping stone. Every crisis presented the opportunity for me to grow in God if I chose to do so.

Every difficult situation creates endless possibilities for God to build character into your life. Godly character is the only thing which can enable you to face life's challenges with joy and confidence. Charisma is not enough.

Storms highlight our weaknesses and strengths so that we can make the changes that are necessary. Sometimes storms highlight our lack of dependence on God. Don't see that as a negative, as something that will disqualify you. See it rather as an opportunity to change. See it as a starting point for the rest of life's journey. When you know where you are, then you know the direction in which you need to go – and that can't be bad!

I believe this is what Jesus was talking about when He said, "You will know the truth and the truth will set you free" (John 8:32). Some of the most needful truth I have had to face up to in my own life was the truth I did not really want to hear about myself.

The truth that Jesus speaks to you is not intended to make you feel condemned or discouraged. He always speaks the truth that will set you free. When He speaks He speaks words that give you hope for the future. He gives you the confidence that you can change, that the circumstances you may be facing right now can and will change. My own testimony is this – when I changed, everything else changed with me.

> *... let us rejoice and exult in our hope of experiencing and enjoying the glory of God. Moreover (let us also be full of joy now!) let us exult and triumph in our troubles and rejoice in our sufferings, knowing that pressure and affliction and hardship produce patient and unswerving endurance. And endurance (fortitude) develops maturity of character (approved faith and tried integrity). And character (of this sort) produces (the habit of) joyful and confident hope of eternal salvation. Such hope never disappoints or deludes or shames us ...*
>
> (Rom. 5:2–5, Amp. Bible)

Get anchored today in the God-kind of hope and let the Lord Jesus Christ build your life into something beautiful and purposeful for Him.

CHAPTER TWO

WORK AND GOD'S PURPOSE

Biography

Anne Atkins works as a writer and journalist and has become one of Britain's most well-known commentators on the subject of today's morals and contributes to panels and debates all around the country. She is married to Shaun and has four children.

She has written three novels. Her first book, *Split Image – Discovering God's True Intention for Male and Female,* is a Biblical study of the roles of the sexes. As a columnist she has written regularly for the *Daily Mail,* and *Mail on Sunday,* as well as the *Daily Telegraph, Guardian, Express* and the *Sun.* She is perhaps best known as the *Telegraph's* weekly Agony Aunt. She contributes regularly to Radio 4's *Thought for the Day,* is currently on ITV's *Sunday Morning* every week and recently presented the *Agony Hour* series for Channel 5.

Most of us in Western society assume a man's first commitment is to his job, and a woman's to her home and children. We are largely intolerant of the sexes "swapping roles". Because we live in society we Christians have absorbed its assumptions, but does the Bible teach that there are different roles for women and men?

Before we address the question we must admit that these "traditional" roles are no longer entirely successful. This is not to say that they cannot be, but they do present us with serious difficulties in the modern world.

If earning a living is to be a man's career it is easy to prepare him for it. He will probably marry and support a family but it does not matter if he chooses not to do so.

If running a home and rearing children is a woman's natural sphere she should be prepared for it too. She will be given an education, but her schooling is not seen as so important or vocational as a boy's. A man is to be her ticket to success: without him, she cannot do *real* woman's work.

Now suppose she gets married, and starts a family. Naturally, she invests more of herself in her marriage than her husband does. His work is to be a success outside the home. Her employment, though, depends on him; her marriage is vital to her work. This puts pressure on them both. He has to make an effort to make a fuss of her. She must try not to be jealous of his time. When the children are born she has her own work – as he has his. The serious problems start when their youngest leaves home. Suddenly she faces virtual lifetime unemployment.

Another girl may not have "made it" at all. Like her sister, she wanted to marry. Unlike her brother, she was unable to do anything about her ambition. She had to wait for her work to materialise. It never did. She is not only a failure, she is a woman doing third-rate men's work.

For if homemaking and childrearing are a woman's work, marriage becomes her aim. Not only can this put a strain on married women, but also on unmarried ones, on those who cannot have children, or those whose children leave home. A man can do a man's work all his life. We have enslaved women in a situation from which Paul says he wanted them freed (1 Cor. 7:32, 34–5).

If a woman prepares for domesticity she may be disappointed. If she prepares for "man's work", and succeeds, she must either forgo a lifelong partner and children or her work. If she decides on some kind of compromise she may be mediocre in both roles.

In addition, our society offers those who work outside the home an increasing variety of choices. By and large, the harder the jobs are to do or get, the more money they bring with them and the higher their status. However, a housewife receives no pay and the status is almost nil. And "woman's work" can be lonely. As Genesis 2 makes clear, for most of us work needs to be a social thing. Housewives work with no one but their children and Hoovers. Housewives can mix together, but they do not work together.

This analysis may seem simplistic and old-fashioned. Many girls are successful and accomplished. Many men do household work. But there is still more of a stigma attached to spinsters than bachelors, and to unemployed men than women.

Many women are torn between work and home. They may find a single life difficult: society persuades them they have "failed". They can find married life worse: they may be given low status, or doomed to mediocrity in the office. On paper we may have sexual equality. In reality, it is difficult for women to work alongside men.

These problems do not mean that we can necessarily abandon the roles. If they are the biblical pattern, we must embrace them, but also make them work. However, there is one more objection: under the present system many areas of work are dominated by one sex. This does mean the sexes depend on one another, which is biblical; but it also means we are often segregated, which is not biblical. Men work largely with other men; housewives work on their own. The work is bound to be impoverished. Governments are run along masculine lines. Homes are dominated by femininity. Business standards conform to men's ideas. Children are moulded and shaped by women.

But we must return to the question. Are these supposedly "traditional" gender roles designed by God? You may "feel" this question is right; if pressed further, you may say it is "natural". Our feelings often tell us when something is right or wrong. On the other hand, they can also easily lead us astray. If you are angry with someone it may feel right to hit him: this is also "natural", but it is seldom right. The fact that we are moral beings means we are capable of moral decisions. What exactly do we mean when we say it is "natural" for women to rear children and to run the home?

We may mean "natural" is what the animals do. The fact that females of many species totally ignore their young, while in others it is the males who look after them, is overlooked. However, amongst non-human primates, the group of species considered nearest to our own, the care of the individual infants is almost exclusively the work of the mother.

Does it mean it is "natural" for us too? But male gorillas and chimpanzees do not provide for the females or the young and do not recognise their own offspring. And why should we choose to copy the apes? Whereas apes are promiscuous, swans show a lifelong faithfulness to their mates – yet share the care of the young equally between cob and pen. The trouble is, of course, we are turning God's creation upside down if we decide what is right or wrong on the basis of animal behaviour, like a parent asking a baby for moral guidance.

What is "natural" could also be understood to be what human societies do. If women look after children in every culture perhaps we can conclude that it is natural because it is universally practised, and therefore essentially human. But, for example, Alaskan Eskimos share the care of the children equally between mother and father. And which particular "universal" or "natural" trends are right? Aggression and greed are found in almost every culture, but it is foolish if we Christians take our standards from non-Christian cultures. We are "not of the world" (John 17:16). This does not mean that we are not to be involved with this world, but we do not have to take our standards from it.

The third possible meaning of "natural" is what our bodies can teach us. What does biology tell us? That one man and one woman are necessary for conception. And that a woman will bear, give birth to, suckle, and incidentally quite often die from the birth of a baby. That is all. It does not tell us who will clean the house, or change the nappies, nor bring home the bacon. We assume that the parent that bears the child must do all the other things for it because that is how our society is structured, and that the other parent will earn money. Neither of these norms is biologically dictated.

Our biology also tells us a man can father twenty children, by different women. And that a woman can bear children from different men. We are very foolish if we think that because something can be called "natural" it must be right. Of course, the truly natural must have been right, but the whole of nature is now fallen. God has given us a moral law so that we can be freed from our fallen "natures". We are free to make up our own minds on the basis of what the Bible says. The truly natural is the way God intended us to be, not the way we are now.

So does the Bible say certain types of work are more suitable for one sex than the other? Let us define three kinds of work. "Breadwinning" is providing money or its equivalent means to live; Western society has largely considered this to be man's work. "Homemaking " is turning this money into food and a pleasant home; again, in recent history we have considered this to be woman's work. And "childrearing" is easily combined in our society with homemaking but not with breadwinning. So it is also thought to be woman's work. However, until industrialisation, work was not rigidly divided in this way. Many people think these roles are "traditional" but they are not. If they appear to be in the Bible we must examine our interpretation carefully, in case we are making assumptions.

The only biblical passage which might suggest that "breadwinning" is the man's job and "homemaking" and "childrearing" the woman's is the second half of Genesis 3. The woman and the man have disobeyed God's word and He pronounces judgment:

> *The LORD God said to the serpent, 'Because you have done this, cursed are you ... upon your belly you shall go, and dust you shall eat ...' To the woman he said, 'I will greatly multiply your pain in childbearing ...' And to Adam he said ... 'cursed is the ground because of you; in toil you shall eat of it all the days of your life ... In the sweat of your face you shall eat bread till you return to the ground ... you are dust, and to dust you shall return.'*
>
> (Genesis 3:14–19, RSV)

There seems to be an assumption here. The woman is cursed in her sphere, the man in his. Her "labour" is having children. His "labour" is tilling the ground and getting food from it. But if we read the verses more carefully we can see that the expectation is not there at all.

The two curses are not on the woman's and the man's "labour", but on the snake and the ground. The snake's curse is addressed to the snake (vv.14 and 15), and the ground's curse to the man (vv.17–19). The curse on the ground is a curse on us all; and we all die (v.19). It is not a punishment on man in his sphere of work; it is a punishment on us all, simply *addressed* to the man.

The woman, on the other hand, is given a specific punishment. Childbirth will be painful. She will suffer as much as the man from the curse on the ground; in addition, she will suffer her own punishment, presumably because she disobeyed first.

There are two assumptions here. The first is that women have babies. But there is no assumption about housework, cooking, or even childcare. Now, everybody knows women have babies, but it is all the other jobs we are concerned with and there is no mention of them here. God addresses to the man the curse which affects us all. The assumption is that he is responsible. It is because he fell that the whole world is fallen (v.17).

Whatever the implications of this, they are nothing to do with work. We all eat in toil. We all go back into the ground, and return to dust. But there is no assumption that the man does any more work, or that he is going to do any more dying. So there is no suggestion in these verses that "work" is a man's responsibility, and "domesticity" a woman's.

It is often thought that the overall biblical picture is that women run homes and care for children, and men provide for them, roles often vaguely connected with the idea of the man being the "head of the household", but this biblical teaching has nothing to do with breadwinning. So let us see what the Bible says about breadwinning, homemaking and childrearing.

We must immediately acknowledge that a woman who works for a living is not condemned. Lydia was a businesswoman, described as "a dealer in purple cloth ... and a worshipper of God" (Acts 16:14). There is no indication that being a businesswoman and worshipping God are incompatible. Priscilla was a tentmaker (Acts 18:3); she and her husband Aquila were in the trade together; the account specifically says "by trade *they* were tentmakers" (RSV). Again, there is no suggestion this is inappropriate for a wife and a Christian.

Lydia, presumably, provided for her household. Priscilla and Aquila earned money together. These women are in no way criticised; however, neither are they held up as examples for us to follow. Paul says "anyone who does not provide for their own people, and especially their family, has denied the faith and is worse than an unbeliever" (1 Tim. 5:8. I am afraid I have sacrificed English grammar for the sake of a more accurate translation of gender). Usually taken to mean that a man must provide for his family, in the context this meaning is forced.

For one thing the Greek has no suggestion of the sex of the person described. To translate it as "he" is to assume that then as now men were thought of as the providers. A few verses later Paul shows that this is not his assumption. For another, Paul is saying Christians must support widowed mothers and grandmothers (v.4). He is not talking about a man working for his wife and children. Lastly, Paul makes clear that he expects women to provide for their families. "If any woman who is a believer has widows in her family she should help them and not let the church be burdened" (v.16).

But the best example of biblical expectations of a married woman is found at the end of Proverbs (31:10–31, RSV). Called the "good wife", here she is a working wife. Her husband trusts in her "and he will have no lack of gain" (v.11). She buys a field and plants it "with the fruit of her hands", money she has previously earned. She gets up early (v.15), and works well into the night (v.18). The first thing that is said about her is that she is valuable (v.10). The last thing said about her is more noteworthy still. "Give to her the fruit of her hands," says the writer, "and let her works praise her in the gates."

Of course this does not mean careerists are praised and housewives condemned. Nor does it mean women, or men, must rush out to work and leave their children inadequately cared for. The "good wife" did some of her work at home; and besides she had servants (v.15). But it does mean that women, like their husbands, are to support their families.

Which sex, in the Bible, is expected to run the home? There is no doubt that a woman is responsible for the welfare of her children, her guests, and her employees. Again the "good wife" of Proverbs 31 provides for her family and her servants.

Paul is unequivocal about the duties of married women. A widow is not to be supported unless she has performed certain duties, including showing hospitality and bringing up children (1 Tim. 5:10). He goes on to say a married woman should be the head of her household (v.14). To Titus he says young women should be taught to love their husbands and children and to be "home-workers" (Titus 2:5). For some women this probably meant doing every chore themselves, for others it meant ensuring that the work was done by employees or servants.

Like a woman, a man is also to run the home and bring his children up properly (1 Tim. 3:4). Paul specifically says that he is not fit to be an elder unless he copes with his household duties (v.4). This does not necessarily mean each husband and wife must perform identical functions; this depends on the culture and personality, but the point is that both sexes are responsible for the home.

Finally, is the most important job, the care of the children, largely the work of the mother, as our society has for some time assumed? Women are to "bring up children" (1 Tim. 5:10). Men are to manage, or care for, their children (1 Tim. 3:12). Again, we are not told what this will entail, but both are responsible.

However, it is in the Old Testament that we find more teaching about mothers and fathers. They are mentioned together, or in the same way: "honour your father and mother, so that you may live long in the land ..." (Exod. 20:12). Both are to be given honour and respect (Lev. 19:3). Both parents teach and instruct their children (Prov. 1:8). If anything is equally shared between the sexes it is the duty of being a parent, although this does not necessarily mean both parents do the same for their children or even spend the same amount of time with them.

There is no suggestion, when we are told to multiply and subdue the earth (Gen. 1:27), that one job (multiplication) is the responsibility of one sex, and the other (subduing) the responsibility of the other. There is no biblical reason why the woman should wash the clothes, or why the man should earn the higher or only income. In fact these ideas are responsible for many men's abdication from their God-given work of running their homes and caring for their children, and for many women's feelings of guilt at their natural desire to work and provide for their families.

Before we conclude there are important things which must be said about our labour. We are all created to work. So we all have a duty to work – but not a duty, or indeed a right, to a *career*. This is totally unbiblical. Plenty of men have sacrificed their families to their careers. If women start doing the same, they will merely be adding one disaster to another.

As we have seen, there are different kinds of work, paid (breadwinning) or unpaid (homemaking, childrearing, and, of course, voluntary work). Our society has equated "work" with breadwinning, the distinction made not between work and idleness, but between pay and lack of it – a disastrous attitude. Those who fail to earn are made to feel unproductive. The "unemployed" must be supported in any work they do and, increasingly, housewives also need support. Women who stay at home to raise a family often suffer depression brought on by low self-esteem, fatigue, loneliness and frustration. Christians must never allow housewives, the unemployed or the retired to feel inadequate or guilty because they are not being paid.

The most significant implication is the wide range of choices we have. My brother tells me that where he lives (amongst Oxford intelligentsia) it is not really acceptable for a young mother to stay at home. Where we used to live (North London suburbia) it was barely acceptable to do anything else. These expectations are not necessarily biblical, and when we realise this we can cease to be dictated to by them.

Some friends of ours had postponed the idea of children because the husband had been hoping to study. Now he would not be able to do the course for several years. Should they wait to start a family or contemplate it now? They were put off by the uncertainty of his job. But, as a doctor, her job is secure. So, if he is still working when the baby is born she can either leave medicine and become a housewife, or stay at work and employ a nanny. If he loses his job, he will be free to look after the baby while she works.

This latter choice had not occurred to them, although it is just as much his job as hers to bring up the family, and as much her job as his to provide for them. Of course this choice has its hardships. Society does not encourage the option and Christians may not be supportive either: some will tell him that he is abdicating from his "headship". And he will need support and encouragement from his partner, just as many women do.

Another couple we know, both highly qualified, have made the conventional choice: she is a housewife and his work continues as before. Temperamentally they are well suited to this, yet this too is not without its difficulties. She will never again be as high-powered as he. He may not be as close to the children as she. They have halved their income and she will need appreciation and company from him.

It is not always necessary for either parent to be the sole housewife. A lecturer at a theological college near us shares her job with her husband: both enjoy the wide variety of work, the children (and the college) are getting the benefit of both, including the different contribution each sex brings to a job;

and they will be able to understand each other's setbacks and joys at work. There are many possible combinations, and we often give ourselves unnecessary problems by conforming to certain patterns.

We have not looked at the question of nannies and childminders. The Bible does not tell us much about them but, despite this, many people think parents who employ help are abdicating from their responsibility. This may sometimes be the case but is not necessarily so. There are three important points.

First, it is preferable and biblical for parents to be the main influence on their children. This is a God-given responsibility, and for those of us with children it is perhaps our most important work.

Second, parents are never going to be the only influence on their children: grandparents, godparents, teachers and society itself are also responsible. The good parent is not necessarily the one who minimises other influences but the one who chooses them with great care. The same applies to nannies, au pairs and childminders.

Third, being a good parent cannot necessarily mean being a full-time one. A man can be a superb parent even if he only spends evenings and weekends with his children; the same must also be true of a woman. So it is perfectly possible for parents to employ help in caring for their children and still to be the best of parents.

Christians sometimes talk about "different roles" for the sexes. People are either vague about these roles or else claim, as biblical, certain rather dated cultural trends. But "roles" is a misleading word. Some people mean we have different contributions to make. This is absolutely true. But other people mean we have different jobs to do. This is false. Except for those which are biologically defined in reproduction, the Bible does not suggest different work for the sexes, although the ways of doing the tasks may be different.

ॐ

Extracted from *Split Image*.
Copyright © 1998 Anne Atkins
Edited and reproduced by permission
of Hodder and Stoughton Ltd.

CHAPTER THREE

GROWING IN THE SHELTER OF GOD'S LOVE

Jeannette Barwick

Biography

Following a career in publishing Jeannette Barwick worked as a Product Manager with an international organisation. She then led a Church community outreach project for many years. Jeannette joined the CWR team in 1984 and is now Special Ministries Manager for CWR (Crusade for World Revival), based at Waverley Christian Centre in Farnham, England.

She coordinates Selwyn Hughes' ministry in the UK and overseas, and as part of CWR's training programme teaches on temperament differences, introducing the Taylor-Johnson Temperament Analysis and the Myers-Briggs Type Indicator to several courses.

Over her many years with CWR, she has developed CWR's Ministry to Women – an aspect of the work very close to her heart. From teaching on the women's residential weekends at Waverley, this ministry takes her to cities around the UK and to many countries overseas. She finds it thrilling to see how teaching on life and relationships from a biblical perspective can be embraced by women of any culture. Jeannette has two daughters who are both married, and treasures her time with them and her two grandchildren.

" Early influences affect us greatly" say the psychologists. The home in which we are brought up has a lot to do with the formation of our outlook on life, our ability to relate to others, and so on. My developmental years were lived out in the atmosphere of a Christian home where God was honoured and worshipped. I am grateful to God for this privilege for I can see, as I look back, how many good and positive things came out of it that have stood me in good stead throughout my life.

Some of these things were: a clear concept of God, a healthy respect for the Bible and sound life values. Take first my concept of God – one of the things I have come to realise is that, throughout the years of my life, the view that I have held of God in my heart is that of a loving, concerned and caring heavenly Father. I am convinced that this was built into me through my relationship with my earthly father. In my work as a counsellor I have often seen that negative earthly relationships, particularly a girl's relationship with her father, can result in a poor view of God. How glad I am that in my developmental years my concept of God was fashioned in the climate of good family relationships.

The Bible was a central dynamic in my home. In my teen years my father ran a Bible class at the church where we all – my mother, father and elder brother – worshipped, and part of my responsiblity was to play the piano for these regular weekly meetings. During the time I participated in the Bible class, the evening programme involved what was described as Bible searching. Bible searching meant looking for a given verse and the first person to find it stood up and read it aloud. Through this method I learned over many years my way around the Bible. I got the feeling in those years that the Bible was different from every other book and, by way of osmosis, the love that my father had for the Bible entered into me.

My clear sense of life values and ethics came directly, I believe, from my mother. I think of values such as fairness, justice, kindness, right living and the keeping to God's commandments. Clear guidance was given, not in an authoritarian way, but gently and lovingly and now, as I look back, I can see how well my mother laid down in the foundations of my personality a sense of ethics and morality.

I suppose much of this came home to me in more recent years as I undertook training in some of the psychological tests which I administer at Waverley Abbey House in CWR's training programme for counsellors. A lot of our psychological make-up comes about through nature but a lot, too, comes from nurture. Out of the climate of a God-fearing home came a richness and an empowerment that have acted as anchors in my life.

After leaving school and college, I went to work in the publishing business and, four years later, in the fashion world. Once again as I look back I can see how God prepares us for the future by taking us through experiences that build into us qualities, skills and characteristics that later become part of our life message. I can trace my Father's hand very clearly in these first few decades of my life as I learned from secular sources things that later on have become a tremendous help to me in the niche into which God has now placed me.

Many people think they are in a siding when they long to be on the main line working for God. But preparation is part of God's great purposes and sometimes the preparation is slow and unhurried. I wonder how Jesus felt when He knew as a boy of 12 that He was called to His Father's business, yet it wasn't until 18 years later that He emerged on to the scene as a preacher and worker of miracles.

I was married in 1964 and four years later I left work in order to have my first daughter – Joanne. Twenty-one months later her sister Katy was born. Both girls are now happily married and I have many good memories of the years when they were small. It was during the early years of my marriage that I came to know Jesus Christ as my personal Saviour. I met some friends who seemed to relate to Jesus in a way I did not know and, with their encouragement, I opened my heart in a more personal way to God and asked Him to fill me with His Holy Spirit. From that day to this my faith has thrived and sustained me in a way for which I am deeply thankful to God.

While my marriage was in its second decade, and my daughters were still young, my husband left me to live with another woman. This, as you can imagine, left me feeling heartbroken and devastated. A broken marriage is, as many in today's world will know, a painful and heartwrenching experience. How does one cope with a failed marriage? Not easily. Tears help. The Scriptures tell that God bottles our tears. Heaven must have many bottles containing my tears. People help too – it's quite amazing how God sends people at the right time when we are in pain and, although they do not always say the right things, the fact that somebody cares can be immensely encouraging.

I found also that giving myself in service to others was a panacea for my pain. I was already involved in the leadership of a mother and toddler group in my local Methodist Church – an outreach into the local community. It became a large and thriving group to which the local social and health workers would bring needy mothers for care and attention. We held small evangelistic meetings and began a Bible study group for new converts. Serving others in this way helped to assuage the hurt.

When my marriage broke up there came a critical moment when I felt an utter failure and unworthy of doing anything for the Lord. My minister helped me by listening with kindness and concern and then encouraged me to continue with the ministry to mothers, which was called the "Oasis Project". Children can be the most wonderful therapy and sometimes playing with them enabled me to forget my personal pain, albeit temporarily. Friendships were forged in those days that still stand today. Other mothers, too, were going through traumas and difficulties and, as we supported one another and reached out in desperation and simple faith to God, He wonderfully met with us and brought us through to a new place with Him.

When people are in pain it draws out from other Christians a desire to help but the help they give, though often sincerely directed, is not always the best. We are so used to giving Bible texts to people hoping they will help, but sometimes this has the opposite effect. I think of a person I heard about who was struggling with anorexia nervosa and was given this text: "Your body is the temple of the Holy Spirit". Then these words were added: "So you should not starve yourself; you should eat." It's so easy to put a Bible text on someone like a band-aid and slap it on a huge gaping wound. Selwyn Hughes calls this the "Evangelical Disease" – using Bible texts as a substitute for gentle, loving and caring words. At this time someone gave me a scripture from Isaiah 54:5, "Your Maker is your husband" to comfort me. It failed to comfort me. Yes, the presence of my heavenly Father was precious to me – please do not misunderstand me – but I didn't want a heavenly husband at that time: I still loved my earthly husband and wanted him to return.

As time went on it was clear that he was never going to come back to the family home. Slowly, however, ever so slowly, I have come to see and recognise that, though the ache for a close human relationship, such as exists between a husband and wife, never goes away, it is possible to have a relationship with the Lord that, though not the same as an earthly relationship, enables you to go on and function with a degree of inner security that is quite amazing. We have been separated for close on twenty years, but we are not divorced.

Although I do not believe God allowed my marriage to break up in order to make me more dependent on Him (as some believe), I am convinced that the brokenness that took place in my soul has been used by God to enable me to reach out with greater understanding to others.

I have always loved those passages in the Gospels that talk about Christ taking bread in His hands and the interesting thing is that whenever He did that He always blessed it then broke it. There is something in us that recoils from brokenness, but often this is the way to a deeper knowledge of God. Like everyone else I shrink from life's breaking experiences, but I have learned that brokenness often leads to greater blessing. Would I have chosen a broken marriage as the route to a deeper knowledge of God and the joy I now experience? No. But in looking back I am glad that, although God did not arrange these difficult circumstances, He has definitely worked through them. I count on His promise in Romans 8:28 that "in all things God works for the good of those that love him."

One of the great movements of God in my life was His leading me into Crusade for World Revival. As my daughters became older it became clear to me that it was right for me to look for a job. I applied to the Methodist Church Headquarters as I had been a member of my local Methodist Church since I was fourteen, and was offered a position to work in the office for those candidating for the ministry. However, as I prayed through my response with my prayer partner, I did not feel God's leading to accept this position. The very same day my attention was drawn to the fact that there were some vacancies at CWR and, with the encouragement of my daughters, I applied for the position of receptionist. I felt an immediate witness that God was in this and the next day I took my application in person to the CWR offices which were then in Hersham, Surrey, a distance of about ten minutes from my home. To my disappointment they were closed for the Christmas holidays. I couldn't find their letter box so I put my letter under the office door. I heard later that at that time (1984) CWR had received about 30,000 applications for their *Through the Bible Every Day in One Year* reading programme, which meant that there were dozens of sacks of mail to be sorted and had I posted my letter it might not have been read for weeks.

Within ten days I was on the staff of CWR. I quickly settled into my work as receptionist and found I was amongst kindred spirits who shared my love of Scripture and the Lord. Within four years of my joining the organisation, Waverley Abbey House was opened by Lord Tonypandy in August 1987. By this time my daughters were completing their education and this left me free to travel the longer distance to Farnham in Surrey each day.

Over the years since I began to work for CWR I have fulfilled a variety of different roles and responsibilities. Prior to the opening of Waverley Abbey House, Selwyn Hughes took me to see the house and where our offices would be. It was on that day that the Lord impressed into my heart the vision for a special ministry to women in the house. A year later, and with the full encouragement of CWR's Executive Directors, we began a programme of events for women which has continued and developed ever since.

My work as Coordinator for Selwyn Hughes' ministry has allowed me to travel to many countries with him and the CWR team. This, in turn, has opened many doors for me to conduct seminars of different kinds alongside the other aspects of the ministry. A particular joy to me has been the women's seminars, and I have been privileged to present these to small and large groups around the UK and in such countries as Uganda, Kenya, Nigeria, Singapore, East and West Malaysia, India and Sri Lanka. One of the highlights of these women's events was the occasion in Nairobi in East Africa, when I addressed a crowd of nearly 3,000 women on the subject of "How to be a Secure Woman". It is a constant delight to me that as I share Biblical principles and deal with relationship issues with women of all ages and different church denominations, cultural differences fade away. The word of God touches us more deeply than any cultural divisions.

One of the joys of my work at Waverley is to organise a regular programme for women, and this ongoing and developing ministry is something for which I continually praise God. There are opportunities for women to draw aside and receive Biblical teaching on subjects of real relevance to their lives, giving a specific women's focus. Everywhere I go I meet women who are busier than ever carrying out multiple tasks and juggling with various roles but, instead of feeling more important as they undertake additional responsibilities, frequently they struggle with a low sense of worth. To see women built up, refreshed and encouraged in the Lord before they return home, gives a great sense of purpose to all that we do. In recent years links have been made with other organisations and we particularly value our partnership with *Woman Alive* magazine.

Oswald Chambers said in one of his books that "life is more tragic than orderly". I have come to see the value of recognising that, although we are Christians, we are not immune to the problems and difficulties that can assail the human condition. In 1998 I was diagnosed with cancer of the colon and the discovery of this came at a time when I was in the midst of a very busy programme. An operation was recommended by my specialist and carried out two weeks later.

Cancer is a very frightening word with a dynamic all of its own. I was shocked when I heard the news but was still aware that God was very near to me. I awoke in the night focusing on a major concern – not "Would I die" but "Would I lose my hair?" At times like this we find out where our priorities lie! Seven months of chemotherapy followed the operation, but it was the kind of future preventative programme which did not involve hair loss. I was very thankful.

It was a great consolation to me that others were able to carry out my engagements during the months following the surgery. How important it is that we do not consider ourselves indispensable. God had others who would fulfil His plans and purposes in my place at that time. After the operation and several weeks of convalescence I was able to return to work and take up my responsibilities once again. This included a significant overseas programme, which involved travelling to the USA, the Phillipines, Singapore and Malaysia, Ghana and Nigeria, India and Sri Lanka in the following months. My treatment was fitted around my travel schedule.

During my convalescence God used two special channels in particular to minister His life and encouragement into my heart. The first was the people of God from all around the world who expressed to me their love and prayerful concern in many different ways. Included amongst them were, of course, my own family, who were quite marvellous in their support, and my two grandchildren, Daniel and Alisha who, though they were only four and two years old, knew of my condition and prayed and shared their love for me, which came across in a deeply healing way.

The other was from the world of nature in the form of a pair of swans who chose to nest on the river bank beneath my kitchen window. My friends at *Woman Alive* magazine sent me an encouraging scripture verse taken from Ruth 2:12 that reads, "May the Lord repay you for what you have done. May you be richly rewarded by the Lord, the God of Israel, under whose wings you have come to take refuge". That Scripture and the image of nestling under His wings brought home to me the reality of God's overshadowing presence. I felt calm and relaxed as the truth became a reality to me, reinforced by what was happening day by day, week by week and month by month under my kitchen window. The faithful care of the swans first for the eggs, then the tiny cygnets, right through to full-grown maturity was one of God's lovely ministrations to me that assisted my healing over the months.

God has used this experience not just to restore me to physical health, but to touch every other area of my life as well. He has wonderfully strengthened and refreshed me spiritually and emotionally too. How I thank and praise Him for His intimate care and love and for the deeper relationship with Him that has ensued.

As we look to the future, in the light of God's past faithfulness, there is one certainty: our God has so much more to give and so much more to draw from us than we can yet imagine.

May Jesus himself and God our Father, who reached out in love and surprised you with gifts of unending help and confidence, put a fresh heart in you, invigorate your work, enliven your speech.

(2 Thess. 2, *The Message*)

CHAPTER FOUR

TEAMWORKING WITH GOD

Fiona Castle

———— ✣ ————

Biography

Fiona married Roy Castle in 1963. She then gave up her work in show business and spent time travelling with Roy as he performed around the world. In 1965 their first baby, Daniel, was born. Julia, Antonia and Ben were to follow.

Sadly, in 1994, after 31 years of marriage, Roy lost his fight against lung cancer. Since his death Fiona continues to work with the Roy Castle Cause for Hope Foundation, raising funds to support the world's first lung cancer research centre.

She is the author of *Give us this Day* and *No Flowers…Just Lots of Joy*, which tell of her tremendous courage at the time of Roy's illness and her subsequent bereavement. Both books are published by Kingsway. She has also written *Rainbows Through the Rain*, published by Hodder & Stoughton.

My mother was very keen on "first impressions". She taught me that I should keep my house immaculate in case people visited. What if the vicar called and there were bits on the carpet? Since then I have always associated vicars with messy carpets! The truth is, the vicar would probably be relieved to see bits on the floor. It's one lesson I've learned, that people are more relaxed if the house isn't perfect. We put great expectations on ourselves for no reason.

But that and other lessons take a long time to sink in. Before I married, my mother said: "Don't come running to me with your problems once you're married because I'll send you running back." She coped throughout the war, provided for dozens of people in our home, looked after the surgery for my father who was a doctor and brought up four children. So I, too, wanted to be the ideal wife and mother. I was also educated at an extremely strict boarding school where the discipline was more suited to training for the SAS than for a dancing career! The standards set were impossibly high. That stood me in good stead in some ways, helping me to be "tough" in times of crisis, but it added to my perfectionist streak.

Eventually, of course, it all started falling apart around my ears. My husband, Roy, was often away when the children were young, and coping alone was very hard. Despite trying my best to make my husband happy and bring up perfect children, I began to see that it was impossible. I was living a make-believe life, hiding behind a mask in an attempt to be accepted by others. I wanted to be the person who could say "yes" to anything, to be admired. Then I could pat myself on the back. It was all to do with pride, trying to build up my low self-image by projecting another image to others. It takes great courage to say "no" under that self-imposed pressure.

I was terrified that if I let go of the reins and revealed the truth about myself, I would lose control completely. I had to have everything just right for when Roy came home and would get up before dawn and go to bed at three o'clock in the morning in order to catch up. But my stomach continually churned with anxiety. I became depressed and irritable. I wouldn't talk to Roy or anyone else about how I felt, but pulled a blind down to stop people getting to the real me. I was totally irrational. Anything Roy tried to say was wrong so he just left me alone and hoped I would come round. I usually did but this all brought terrible stress and tension within the home, just the opposite of what I was striving for.

I became a Christian after Ben, my youngest child, was born and I was absolutely at rock bottom. A friend led me to the Lord and, although the circumstances hadn't changed, I knew I definitely had. As soon as I had prayed "the prayer", I sensed an inexplicable peace inside me. All that churning anxiety seemed to melt away and instantly I felt free to go back home and begin living differently. I realised that Jesus had released me to live a life pleasing to Him and not just to fulfil the expectations of others – a gift of revelation which I sorely needed and which transformed our home life.

I didn't go home and blurt it all out to Roy. I wanted him to see me changing in my attitudes towards him, the children and the home. Gradually, things got better and better, especially as his faith grew too and we began to walk the journey together. I knew then I didn't have to get in a state if things didn't go my way. I wasn't going to fall apart if I made mistakes or couldn't keep up with everything. I had new weapons to deal with the self-pity which led to my depression. No longer was I saying: "Poor me, everyone thinks I've got a great life and no one understands what I'm going through." I began to share any discouragements with Roy and discovered that communication was the key. Explaining how I felt over a cup of tea released so much of the tension and he was able to help me.

I began to see that I had often used my "depression" as something to hide behind, so that people would make allowances for me and I didn't have to get on with life. I remember hearing someone speaking about the man at the pool of Bethesda. Jesus tackled him about his complaint that he never got near the healing pool because everyone else beat him to it. "Do you really want to get well?" Jesus asked. Sometimes, if we're honest, the answer is no, we would rather stay as we are, attracting attention that way. I knew that's what I was doing. I needed to learn how to share my disappointments and failures with other people and to get help.

Women, particularly as new Christians, need so much support. The friend who led me to the Lord was older and she nurtured me. I could ring her up and ask how to handle a situation. We could do so much more to encourage each other in this way within the church. As mothers and wives, we have to cope with so many issues, not just big problems but all the small, tricky dilemmas we experience. We need each other's wisdom and encouragement.

I began to meet with a group of three friends each week after I was converted. One of us would look after all the children while the others went off on their own to do something for themselves. Time off is a lifesaver, even if it's only once a week.

It's something to look forward to and reminds you that you are a unique person. We can become submerged in the role of "mum" and those years at home with young children can be the loneliest times of our lives. The jobs we do are humdrum and repetitive. It can seem as if the only time our hard work is recognised is when we've forgotten to do something!

I have travelled a lot, but I always wanted to stay connected to the local church and this has been so valuable. I have maintained a couple of regular commitments consistently, because I wanted to stay in touch with people, to know what's happening in their lives. It's anchored me to the local fellowship and made me accountable.

I help with a young mothers group which meets at the church once a week. We provide carers for their children and give them an opportunity to be built up and affirmed. I'm a Methusaleh of mums now compared to many of them, but I love to reach out to them. Many spend long days alone or have only just moved to the area from London, giving up their careers to start families. It can be alarming to find how much time a new baby takes up and I know from my own experience how easily things fall apart.

I am passionate in my conviction that those years at home, however difficult, are vital for the family's sake. This is why I am so keen to affirm women who make that choice. As society puts increasing pressure on women to get out to work, earn more money and own more things, being a stay-at-home mum can feel like a second-rate job. Women receive affirmation at work from their job descriptions, but being a mum is the most important job a woman can do. You can have a job which is high-powered and financially rewarding, but if the firm goes bust or you get made redundant, all your hard work is forgotten within a few days. But the parental role has an effect well after the children have left home!

My personal view, therefore, is that a mother will never regret staying at home to look after the children. We only get one shot at parenting. I know that it can't always be possible, for lone parents or those who have to work because their husband can't. But sometimes the pressure to provide our children with wonderful toys, holidays and gadgets influences us to believe that we must earn enough to support it all. I know my opinions swim against the tide to some extent, but I wonder whether our expectations are far too high. We need to work hard to keep our families together, even if less money means moving to a smaller property or tightening the budget. Keeping up with the Jones's is just something we do for our own pride and satisfaction. It doesn't do anything for our families' happiness.

The rise of feminist attitudes has a lot to answer for and I think we can be easily influenced by them. This kind of thinking puts Christian women in a difficult position as the differences between the teaching of the church and the "wisdom" of the world become more apparent. My heart goes out to young Christian girls who want to save themselves for marriage but find it almost impossible to meet young men who understand that. Right from the age of twelve or thirteen, the girls are having to stand out in the crowd, just what they don't want to be doing at that age!

This issue of women's rights can affect the Christian home. I know that when Roy was away so much it was so difficult not to "take over". I ran the house, I made the decisions, I disciplined the children. Effectively, I usurped Roy's position in the home, but I didn't realise this until I became a

Christian. I had to redress the balance, because I knew things were not running on God's principles. As I changed, I found myself in a place of incredible peace and, surprisingly, protection and security.

Obviously, it was not always possible for Roy to be there to administer discipline. He used to say: "I can't come home and be mad at the children just because you've had a hard time with them!" In fact, Roy found it difficult ever to be cross and I had to stifle giggles if he got into a temper; it was so unusual. Once, Anto, my daughter, had done something very naughty, I can't remember what. When Roy got home I just handed it over to him and told him to deal with it, I'd had enough. Apparently (and I only found this out from one of my sons after Roy had died) Roy went to Anto and said: "Mum says you've been very naughty and that I've got to be very cross with you. So if she asks you, I have!"

This issue of Biblical submission is so easily misinterpreted, especially in the light of feminist thinking. I think it's a matter of teamwork, not domination by either partner. But women now are so busy trying to assert themselves, to have a voice, to be respected in the workplace and at home. We are always hearing how much more intelligent women are than men or how much more efficient. Of course women don't want to be labelled "doormats", but it also means that marriage becomes a competitive environment and the children suffer.

We should try to accept the God-given differences between men and women. People might say this was old-fashioned, but I don't remember Roy ever doing the ironing or the washing up. I felt that my role was to do these things because Roy worked hard to provide for the family and I was there to support that and create a comfortable home for him on his return.

Communication is vital. Resentment breeds easily when we keep our irritations to ourselves. Roy and I learned to discuss things and to keep the communication open and honest. We used to take time to be together, walking or playing squash, so that we had a chance to be away from the telephone and the demands of the family. It is so easy, as a couple, to find yourselves not necessarily arguing but running on parallel lines and never communicating properly. The husband does his work and you do yours and then you both collapse into bed, exhausted, not really reaching out to each other. Finding opportunities to have "eyeball to eyeball" talk with Roy made a lot of difference. It meant that we could explain how we felt to each other. For instance, disagreements can turn into rows if you can't find a way of expressing your feelings respectfully. We can learn to say: "Look, the way you said that really hurt me. Could you say it in a way which doesn't make me feel put down?"

When making decisions, I think it is vital to defer to one another, to respect one another's opinions and gifting. It may well be that, for instance, the wife finds dealing with finance easier because she trained as an accountant! The danger is that she berates her husband for being useless with money and puts him down. In this situation, why can't they work as a partnership? She could deal with the finances under his leadership, checking things through with him to make sure he is happy with the way she is handling it.

The Proverbs 31 wife sets us an example. Her husband doesn't resent the fact that she has bought a field or used her resources to give to the poor, but he blesses her. She is submissive, but creative and wise with it, a woman who knows her role and purpose in life and fulfils it with the approval of her husband. We know that women can hold a child under one arm, stir a pot with the other and answer the telephone at the same time! But that's in our genes and men are made differently. It's not something for us to use against our husbands. The irony is that, if a woman goes out to work all day and comes home when her husband does, it's often she who notices which jobs need doing anyway. Most men aren't programmed to see that the house needs dusting!

It's very important for a woman to develop interests of her own, especially if she feels isolated. It can be vital when the children have left home to have something to be involved in. When my children were younger, I took on speaking engagements within school hours so that the children weren't affected. Roy often commented that I would never have the "empty nest syndrome" because I had an interest of my own. I've appreciated his words, because now I am a widow I have a life and a purpose. It's not that I don't notice his absence, but it gives me something to get up in the morning for. It makes me busy, and I would rather it was this way round than be searching for things to fill my time.

I do appreciate, though, how easy it is to become too busy. The only way I avoid this is to stay close to God, to meet with Him regularly and ask Him what He wants from me. I get my sense of purpose and identity from these times with Him and from reading the Bible. I find great inspiration from the Psalms, especially if I'm feeling low, and I think the book of Ephesians is so good. If we only had that one book and lived by it things could be very different. These times with God provide guidance for me, then I can be wise about when to say "no". Selwyn Hughes says that if you find you are too busy, you are obviously busier than God wants you to be. Obviously, you can't not be busy if you have children; running them to school and back and keeping the house in some sort of order takes up a lot of time. I still think we need to take stock regularly. If your stomach starts churning, as mine does when I get over-committed, it's time to stop and think. I was no good to anybody when I was in a state of constant panic.

The peace God gave me when I first became a Christian has always been my yardstick. If I feel that disappearing, I know something's wrong and I recommend it as a surefire way to diagnose when you're overdoing it. The friend who led me to Jesus told me that God would give me all the time I needed to do what He wanted me to do and I have put that into practice and found it true. If the Hoover doesn't come out of the cupboard or the washing isn't done, what does it matter as long as the children can come home and get a cuddle from Mum? They don't care about your inefficiency and neither does the Lord. He loves you for who you are, not what you get done.

It is so tempting to put a low value on yourself, it's such an insidious attitude. Recently I found myself picking out the bad fruit from the fruit bowl. I'll eat that apple with the brown bit because I know no one else will and somehow I don't consider myself worth a decent apple! When Roy was away I would cook fishfingers for the children and finish up their leftovers, simply because I didn't consider myself worth cooking for.

But God thought I was worth dying for. That's how much He values me. There are so many times when we feel unappreciated by others around us. Our sense of uniqueness comes from His love for us, and staying close to Him is the only way to preserve it.

This chapter was written by journalist
Fran Hill, after an interview with Fiona Castle.

CHAPTER FIVE

PRESENT YOUR LIFE

Margaret Ellis

Biography

Margaret Ellis is a former history teacher and is one of the leaders of Revelation Church in Chichester, linked with the Pioneer network of churches. She has a preaching ministry, but in particular loves working with individuals to see broken lives restored and people released in areas of ministry.

She is training as a counsellor in order to be able to work professionally in the future with people who have been abused.

Margaret is married to Roger and they have two young children.

Sitting on my bed, tears streaming down my face, I called my parents in. I handed them a note I wanted them to have after I had died. They needed to know that I willingly gave my life, but that I loved them. I was worried how they would cope.

I was the grand age of ten years old, and had been praying and reading from Romans 12:1, "I appeal to you, therefore, brothers and sisters, by the mercies of God, to present your bodies as a living sacrifice, holy and acceptable to God, which is your spiritual worship" (RSV). Full of missionary stories in my head, I believed God was calling me to martyrdom. With anguish, I wrestled with my inner thoughts, surrounded by my teddy bears, as well as that great cloud of witnesses spoken of in Hebrews 12!

I am grateful to my parents that they did not belittle my childish belief. Looking back, I believe Father God was laying an important foundation in my life.

As I grew up, I found it hard to know where I fitted. In my class at secondary school there seemed to be two options: either to go around with the "horsey" set or the "discos and make-up" set. I hated snobbery, so that ruled out the horse-riding brigade, and I felt uneasy with the sexual adventures of the other set. It left me with a handful of other misfits, or to bury myself in my books.

It wasn't a lot better at church. There it seemed there were the "square" ones or the compromised ones. The latter were sleeping around as though it made no difference being a Christian. And the others were experts at being square, boring Christians who couldn't relate to anything or anyone outside the church. I didn't want to compromise, so I hung around the square ones. But it wasn't me, and it left me feeling rejected and insecure. It seemed like I fitted nowhere and this caused emotional scars that I would have to find God's healing for in the future.

The more I read in the Bible and imagined those times, the more I knew there must be something more to life as a Christian that I was missing. I had a wonderful relationship with God on the inside; I knew He could do anything. But it was all locked up on the inside; very little came out and made any difference to the people around me or my own experience of life. I buried myself in my school work, but decided that when my "O" level exams were over I would take the summer to pray for what I was missing.

As part of my summer holidays I went away on a CYFA camp (an Anglican youth camp). There, for the first time in my life, I met other Christians my age who were passionate about their faith but culturally relevant to our generation. There was a group of them from a place called Chichester and I could see they had what I was looking for. I was magnetised by their spiritual verve and their natural evangelism. I was also attracted to a particular long-haired blond extrovert by the name of Roger!

Due to my low self-esteem I presumed he wouldn't be interested in me, but I was wrong. I went down to Chichester to visit, having agreed to go out together. In his charmingly brash way, he dumped me in my first ever charismatic meeting, with no preamble.

I was awestruck at the sense of the presence of God. I heard people speaking in heavenly languages I had never heard before, and I heard God speak prophetically through people there. I felt like Moses standing in front of the burning bush.

This was holy ground. I took my shoes off and trembled as I worshipped my awesome God.

A lady stood up to speak in the meeting. It seemed as though she was describing my spiritual journey to this place. Then she said God wanted to give this person the gift of tongues if they would receive it. I knew it was me. My heart raced and then stopped as the whole meeting waited. What was I supposed to do? She had given no instructions. I was too self-conscious to move. The moment lingered then passed.

I cried myself to sleep that night. Father God had offered me the most precious present and I had thrown it back in his face.

My experiences of not fitting in had left me feeling rejected, lacking in confidence. Although I came first in every school exam, my reports rang like a monotonous church bell: "she lacks the confidence she deserves in her abilities." The truth was that I couldn't believe I was special enough for God to give me something so valuable.

When Roger prayed for me the next day I received three little words in tongues. They were my treasure, my sign that my awesome God could break out from the inside of me to the outside. So began a mind-blowing journey of discovery into God's belief in me that was going to give me the commitment to serve Him.

I was off to boarding school to do my "A" Levels. There was a new freedom inside me to be open about my faith and to use prayer to bring God into other people's lives. I started first with my nine-year-old sister and sent her home speaking in tongues. In the close environment of boarding school many a long night was spent listening to people's fears and needs and respectfully sharing with them my faith in Jesus and how prayer could help.

My holidays were spent down in Chichester with Roger and his friends in the youth group that we named "Revelation" (Revs for short). Roger was into heavy metal music (cool at the time!) and had founded a rock society in Chichester in his pre-salvation days. This became his evangelistic stomping ground and as he shouted the gospel over the volume of the music many others started to follow Jesus too.

The youth group started to grow and, as one by one we were filled with the Holy Spirit, it dawned on us that it would be much more eventful if we worshipped God, than sat around listening to endless records.

We worshipped our hearts out often until the early hours of the morning; singing, shouting, crying ... expressing our youthful wonder at His presence. "Come near to God and He will come near to you" it says in the book of James (4:8). It happened. We did; and God did. His presence was electric, tangible, warm, awesome. I was learning to add a second piston to my spiritual engine: the power of expressing myself to God.

I completed my "A" levels with straight As and won my dream place to Cambridge University. The plan was to take a year off and the family culture was to use this to travel. I would spend a few months in Chichester before I left for Singapore. But God was building a church down there in Chichester and I soon found myself up to my eyes in discipling new converts, preaching and generally helping Roger, who was the main leader of the group.

One night Roger and I had a steaming argument as he challenged me whether it was my pride and ambition that was sending me to Cambridge and to travel, or whether it was God's calling on my life. Deep down I heard God ask me to build his church, to disciple these young people, to lead and teach them. Was I prepared to pay the price? I remembered my death note to my parents. This was the start. And it was hard for them.

During this year we found the courage to call ourselves a church. I stayed in Chichester for the whole of that year, waitressing and then being paid part-time by the others in Revs to give more time to all that needed to be done.

I had a lot to break through in myself to do this work. I still struggled with rejection. I blushed every time I spoke in front of more than two people. Many people belittled us because of our age. The first visiting speaker we ever had told us we "didn't have ten per cent of the material to build a church". Many of the young people becoming Christians had horrendous backgrounds and were very damaged. There were many pastoral problems and little support from anyone outside ourselves. But we learned to lay hold of God, to see the supernatural break out, and to be accountable to each other, learning from and supporting one another.

At the end of my year off I asked God about Cambridge. He said "Go..." but there was no full stop. I was aware that it might not be a finished sentence.

I threw myself into life at university. I loved the studying and enjoyed the social life. I found a good church, although it was strange to be ignored and presumed to be incapable of doing anything in God. I asked God at the end of each term if He was happy with my being there and felt His affirmation. But at the end of the third term I sensed a silence from heaven. As I prayed and fasted I knew it was time to go. This was a bigger test. However, I knew God had spoken and that I could trust Him.

My tutors at Cambridge thought I was mad. My parents were devastated. I didn't know what I would do as "A" levels didn't seem to summon very interesting jobs. Compared to Romans 12, this was nothing. But it was a test: was I prepared to lay my life down to serve what God was doing, was I prepared to sacrifice, was I prepared to break the mould? I was, and I did it.

I found myself walking into Bognor College when out shopping one day. It was a teacher training college in the next town but it turned out they also did a few degrees, including history, which was my subject. By the time I walked out I'd had informal interviews with everybody relevant and had been offered a place without having to repeat the first year.

It didn't quite have the prestige of Cambridge University and the lectures were deadly boring. But God is no person's debtor. I got my degree, did a PGCE (Postgraduate Certificate in Education) and ended up teaching history in one of Chichester's secondary schools, which is what I would have wanted anyway. The other advantage was that I found the work easy, so had plenty of time to help lead the church. It was ideal. There was nothing to hold us back now in our relationship, so Roger and I ended our two-year engagement with a wonderful wedding. The wedding was on a Sunday. We cancelled our normal meeting and the whole church was invited.

After three to four years we had around 120 committed members in Chichester. We believed it was time to plant a church, so sent out a team to the next town of Bognor. Through the subsequent years we planted also in Barnham, Portsmouth and Selsey. We have stayed as one church with different geographical and demographical expressions. Over the years we have been through many changes in how we have structured the church. We have learned to be flexible. We warn new people joining us that our motto is: "Constant change is here to stay!" We are now one church in a region with cells that cluster into groups that look like congregations. I am part of our oversight team supervising all our congregations, but we also have leaders in the localities.

As the original group of us have got older and had children we have not wanted to lose our calling as a church to Generation X. Every few years we have recycled into the next emerging generation: at one stage it was Goths in their black clothes, Doc Martens and whitened faces. Then it was club culture with their dance shoes and music. We now have a youth congregation, whose leadership Roger and I have long since handed over to younger people. But we are there in the background for them, believing in them and encouraging them to present their lives to God as living sacrifices.

It hasn't all been good. After we had only been going as a church for a few years, I had a distraught phone call from a close friend. She had found love letters revealing that her husband was having an affair with a young girl in the church. They were two of our closest friends and had both given much to building the church. We were all devastated. Through a lot of pain, we learned about standing together through these times. We were very much strengthened too by the outside support and advice of Gerald Coates and Ishmael. It was good by then not to be alone as a church.

I spent many a long hour listening to different women's traumas. Many disclosed sexual abuse that they had suffered. We had to find the capacity to be there for people. But there was nothing more fulfilling than watching people grow in strength and freedom, out of their pain.

I also learned the hard way in terms of my capacity. Many times I over-pushed my physical limits. I remember sitting in the staff room one lunch hour, pregnant with our first child, teaching full-time and being the main leader of our Chichester congregation! On two occasions over the years I have ended up with long-term viruses where I couldn't do anything but sleep for around three months. God was gracious and healed me overnight from both of them when He saw fit. But this was after several months of learning lessons the hard way. I probably still haven't fully mastered this lesson yet!

Aside from the difficult times, I was aware that part of my journey was specific to being a woman.

A young male student came up to me, his eyes shining, after I had spoken at his university Christian Union meeting. "I'm amazed," he stammered. "You were really anointed!" I wasn't quite sure how to respond so I just smiled. "I've never heard a woman speak before," he said. "I believed only men could preach. I can't understand that I could feel God's power in your words!"

Other times women would hear me speak and tell me, "You're the best preacher I've ever heard." It was obvious that was a gross exaggeration of objective truth! But I realised I was touching something in them that others couldn't. I was modelling something to them because I was a woman, like them.

Through my study of the Scriptures, I believed I was free to receive God's anointing irrespective of gender, but respecting faith, obedience and character. I wanted to model this for others. As I saw the sexism and oppression of women in the church more broadly when I travelled, I was aware of the privilege of my environment in Revs. From the early years we had laid foundations into the church theologically and relationally that allowed us as women to reach our full potential in God, alongside the guys. The tapes and writings of Roger and Faith Forster and Martin Scott helped us tremendously in this.

My heart is to see all people laying down their lives to paint a section in the masterpiece of the kingdom of heaven. I see so much darkness, despair, meaninglessness. I haven't got a gender agenda. I have never been on a feminist campaign. But I am on a campaign to enlist every man, woman and child to service on God's side in the battle of kingdoms that is raging. I am passionate that this does not allow anyone to be excluded by their sex, their colour, by themselves, by their education, by their brokenness. There is too much to be done. In the words of one of the songs of a band called "Fruit", formed by some of the young people in Revs: "Don't walk blind, into the night, just as if to fade away, and to say you've lived for nothing".

This has at times meant breaking the mould as a woman, often to my amusement! One evening we decided to meet to pray as leaders of our Chichester congregation with the leadership team of one of the local Anglican churches. During a quiet moment, my second child, who was a couple of months old, propelled a projectile vomit over the unsuspecting vicar as he prayed! Fortunately he took it in good spirits!

Over the course of these years I have dreamed of one day having the privilege of being able to focus on some specific area of social justice, instead of being a jack-of-all-trades. One day, a young lady I have loved and cared for through many traumas, disclosed that the cause behind them all was that for many years she had been sexually abused by someone close to her. I kicked myself for having been so blind for so many years that I had not seen this root cause. I understand that this was her time to be ready to tell me. But it motivated me deeply, and made me see all the other issues she struggled with in their true light at last.

There was also another girl I was discipling. She was and is, full of the call of God on her life. One evening she was raped in the road next to where I live. Supporting her, as she chose to report it to the police, impacted me deeply because of the total lack of care and provision for someone in her situation in our town. A few of us were able to care for her as a church; but what if she hadn't been in the church? I realised that there were no specialised services in our town for survivors of sexual abuse. Something tipped inside me like scales. I couldn't hear and know any more without doing something about it.

People were being robbed of their dignity, their human rights. So much damage was being caused. So much evil was being expressed without response. I could see so little justice in the courts. The silent scream has the right to have the volume applied, to be heard, to be believed. Over the years I had seen healing come over time to countless people as they were given emotional visibility, love and prayer. Why should this be locked up in the church?

A dream was formulating to set up a Life Centre in my town that would provide phone crisis lines and face-to-face counselling to anyone who had been raped or sexually abused. I then needed a strategy as to how it might be possible to deliver this dream. I got myself on a two-year counselling course at a local university, as well as on a specialised course in Psychosexual Counselling and Therapy. Alongside these courses I have been trained by and am doing voluntary work for a Rape Crisis Centre in another city.

As I write, I will complete these courses in a few more months. I know I need to be properly trained before I have the right to attempt my dream. I am daunted by the many hurdles on this race course. At times, I feel again as I did fifteen years ago at the age of eighteen that I could drown in lack of confidence internally, or opposition externally. But I remember how Abraham kept pioneering for one hundred years. I know the dream God has put before me this time, and I'm going to run towards it.

I have written this story to encourage you, too, to present your life as a living sacrifice. I have wanted to share some of the lessons I have learned in my journey, in the hope that they will spur you on in yours. In the words of the writer to the Hebrews:

Therefore, since we are surrounded by such a great cloud of witnesses, let us throw off everything that hinders and the sin that so easily entangles, and let us run with perseverance the race marked out for us. Let us fix our eyes on Jesus, the author and perfecter of our faith, who for the joy set before him endured the cross, scorning its shame, and sat down at the right hand of the throne of God. Consider him who endured such opposition from sinful men, so that you will not grow weary and lose heart.

(Heb. 12:1–3)

CHAPTER SIX

GOD IS GOOD FOR WOMEN!

Michele Guinness

———— ❧ ————

Biography

Brought up in a Jewish family, converted as a teenager and married to an Anglican clergyman, Michele Guinness is a freelance journalist and PR consultant. She has worked as a researcher, writer and presenter for most major British television companies and for BBC Radio 2 and 4.

She is currently press officer for the Blackpool, Wyre and Fylde Community Health Services NHS Trust and is involved in communication training.

As well as contributing regularly to a variety of magazines, she has written: *Child of the Covenant*, her autobiography; *Promised Land*, the story of a Yorkshire mining town during the strike; *Tapestry of Voices*, meditations on women's lives; *A Little Kosher Seasoning*, exploring how Christians can discover their Jewish roots; *Made for Each Other: Reflections on the Opposite Sex*, looking at how men and women relate to each other – or don't! And *Is God Good for Women?* tells how twelve women of faith broke through traditional glass ceilings. Her latest book, *The Guinness Spirit*, about her husband's illustrious brewing, banking and missionary ancestors, will be published later this year.

Michele lives in Lancaster and has two children, Joel aged 21 and Abby aged 18.

How good God – the God of Abraham, Isaac, Jacob and Jesus – is for women! Yet both cultures – Jewish and evangelical Christian – have, to a certain extent, missed the point. They both have strengths too: areas where we can encourage each other to fulfil our God- rather than church-given role as women.

My earliest expectations were that I would be a wife and mother. I remember my mother saying to me: "I don't know why we're educating you; you'll only go off and get married and have babies." Yet education for women is part of Jewish heritage: Jewish women were educated, even at the time of Jesus.

Of course, it may seem a stereotypical thing for my mother to say, but to be a wife and mother, for a Jewish woman, means you are literally all powerful – "she who must be obeyed"! My mother ruled in our home, and my father – who was a GP, dispensing health and goodwill all around the community – as soon as he arrived on the doorstep, was completely disempowered. I would see his face change – from authority to subservience. So there is this balance of territory: women are expected to rule in their own area. I fully expected to be all-powerful in my own home.

But it's not just in the home that Judaism expects women to be powerful. Proverbs 31, for example, shows that women have always run businesses. By the time of Jesus, it was quite a custom to have women teachers and women disciples, something many Christians don't realise. So Jesus' value of, and friendships with, women weren't as revolutionary as they seem. We are finding out so much about Jewish culture in New Testament times: half of the New Testament has been closed to many Christians, because of how little we know about daily life and customs at that time.

For instance, men and women sat together in the synagogue. Men were in the Women's Court in the Temple: it wasn't exclusively for women; that was just its name. In fact, women were only exempt from religious practices when they were breast-feeding and needed their energy for their children: women only became excluded from full religious life in the 6th century, about the time Islam came on the scene. We are finding out so much more through archaeology and study: for example, inscriptions have been found on walls reading "Mother of the Synagogue". Who was she? We don't know.

Mary, too, is a much more powerful figure than the one that has been portrayed among Christians. During the wedding at Cana, when the wine runs out, she has authority to tell the servants: "Do whatever he tells you" (John 2:5). She is there at the cross. Years later, after the crucifixion, one of the earliest fellowships met in her home. This is a woman who knows what her life is about, what the pain was for. She must have had a huge influence on the early church.

When I married Peter, we moved to a mining town where the church was very middle-class but, because I was Jewish, from another culture, I could see what was going on. Women were very powerful in this society. Peter's mum had never worked outside the home, but working-class women always had. In these communities, the man came home with his pay packet, handed it to the woman, and was given back his beer money.

During the War, working-class women worked, unless they

were pregnant. Six weeks after you had your baby, there was a knock on the door, summoning you back to the munitions factory. Once the War was over, the men wanted the jobs back. This "women at home" business is such a middle-class thing!

The church is riddled with middle-class culture and, seeing things from a different perspective, I began to wonder what other areas there were where we accept as Christian norms that are just cultural.

In Christian society, it's women who are responsible for the "religious" upbringing of their children, by default – it's not something the men see as their role. Yet that is such a contrast to how I had been brought up. Men were the spiritual leaders then. As a child, I went to Hebrew classes four times a week, plus a two-hour session on Sunday morning, from about age six to age twelve. I was one of the stars of the class, because I loved languages, and I was up there with the local rabbi's son. Then came a point where he was going to sail on ahead and I was going to be left behind – because I was female.

A few years ago, I was asked at church to speak on reading Bible stories to children. However, I realised that, in my home, I had taken on the Jewish role of the mother, encouraging my children by giving them a sense of celebration on the Sabbath and at festivals. Peter looked after their spiritual education.

I very much wanted my kids to grow up as Christians but, early on, I began to realise that traditional, middle-class, evangelical spirituality doesn't work. How do you have a "quiet time" with two kids banging on the door – even the toilet door? Then there is the idea of family prayers. Some Christians have quoted the familiar saying to me: "The family that prays together stays together" (and they say it in such a lugubrious voice!), yet nobody tells you how this works. You can't say to a child "Stop playing, we're going to pray"! Nothing is more guaranteed to put them off God.

The Jewish approach and philosophy is more about finding God in the everyday. Somehow, prayer should be like breathing: if it's not normal for a child, it's not normal. I very much wanted my kids to survive spiritually, so I began to think about the how, and I realised that, as a child, the thing I had loved about Judaism was the colour, the richness, the laughter and the jokes. I began to see that, if I created an "occasion" on the Sabbath eve, every Friday night – lit candles, prayed, prepared special food – it worked like a dream. Now my grown-up children will say to me, "Come on: it's Friday night, let's get ready."

This is so much better than traditional evangelicalism, which seems to have lost its celebration, warmth and colour, and has little community in the Jewish extended family sense – but the spiritual teaching role remained my husband Peter's. He had always done things like reading the Bible with the children, underlining the importance of the man taking responsibility for the children's spiritual welfare.

At our wedding there was a prophecy: "Partings there will be, when the way of the cross demands it." At the time, I wasn't sure what this meant: I remember saying to Peter on our way to the honeymoon: "Are you going to have a travelling ministry?" I gave up work when I married, had my children, then found I was in demand for writing, speaking, radio and TV opportunities, which came with the publication of *Child of the Covenant*. So few Jews were converted then. Then when Abby, our youngest, was five, I was asked to become a researcher at Central TV.

This new role involved a lot of sacrifice. Many times I had to leave the children behind with Peter. Some Christians were shocked, and said, "How can you leave your children?" Women can get censure within the church when we explore a role other than wife and mother.

Yet mothering is for such a very short time. Sure, your grown-up children still need you – once every six months! My son Joel is at Oxford, and he wants me as a walking wallet: it's "Mum, I'm out of money again." We're great friends now, and I love it. Yes, they still need you, but not all the time. We need to be open to God, asking Him, "What do you want of my life – the whole of it?"

The trouble is that, in our society, you become invisible as soon as you push a pram. It wasn't until I was in my 40s that I had the confidence to believe I had something to say and offer as myself – I wasn't just Peter's wife and the children's mother. Women are often blind to the passage where Jesus says that anyone "who loves father and mother more than me is not worthy of me" (Matt. 10:37). They think it's directed at the men, not "me the mother", "me the wife", and "me the person".

God describes us women as man's "helper". The word used, in Hebrew, is *ezer*, the same word used in the well-known phrase "The Lord is my helper" (Heb. 13:6). The popular Christian idea of "helper" is woman in a "supportive" role: a bit like the BAFTA Awards: Best Supporting Actress! But God is a "helper" and He doesn't have a supportive role! Our understanding of the word "help" has gone awry somewhere. This hasn't been helped by the effects of the Fall – men encroaching on women, women using men – or of today's society. The 90s "laddettes" have a lot to answer for. However, the church does tend to be reactionary. Let's look at what the Scriptures say, and intend, for men and women.

When the Scriptures talk of headship, though authoritarianism is going out of society, we take it as a model in church: we superimpose it onto headship. Headship is about accountability: men are accountable to God, to love their wives as Christ loved the church. The role of men in encouraging women is crucial: God wants women, as well as men, whole – as fulfilled as possible. Some men have not seen encouraging women as part of their accountability.

Men can still open doors for women, metaphorically speaking. I am grateful to so many men who have done so for me. While I was writing *Is God Good for Women?* it struck me that there is always, somewhere, a man in a woman's life to affirm her – her father, a brother, a husband.

I adored my father, though when I was born, he had wanted a boy. He even lost a £5 bet over it! But we were always extra close. I was very like him – interested in the same things. Early on, he recognised that education would be important for me. Once he told me: "You could be a doctor one day". A doctor, not a nurse!

As women, we blossom best under the encouragement, the affirmation, of a father, husband, colleague or brother. Men, the greatest gift you can give your daughters is to say "Go for it."

I do think that men can make us feel a million dollars – and help us take risks. Men are traditionally the risk-takers, but Old Testament women like Ruth, Deborah and Hannah took enormous risks. Many times, God calls women to be assertive about their calling: he says "Do it, whatever the risk." A lot of men have to be coerced into doing the will of God! But we can be godly in our assertiveness. Joy Carroll, the priest who proved a role model for the character of Revd Geraldine Grainger in the BBC sitcom *The Vicar of Dibley*, never became a campaigning member of the Movement for the Ordination of Women. "That's not my style," she told me, when I interviewed her for the book *Is God Good for Women?* "I felt I could best bring about change by working within the structures, using the gentle art of persuasion."

Yet, as the youngest-ever member of the General Synod, there came a day when Joy used her gentle, God-given assertiveness. During the debate over "flying bishops" – a measure suggested to cater for those priests refusing to be served by Bishops who had worked with female colleagues – she was moved to protest. "If all this was about provision for people opposed to the ordination of black people, would the Synod be as gracious about it?" she asked a silent Chamber of clergy. "What I'm voting against is inconsistency and bad theology – for fear that the Church may find herself bent so far backwards that she may fall over."

Her speech did not sway the result, but it did hit home with BBC writer Richard Curtis, who had written one episode of *The Vicar of Dibley,* and was looking for more inspiration. He phoned her, visited (bringing Dawn French with him), and based much of his writing in future episodes of the hugely popular sitcom on this energetic, attractive, engagingly "normal" member of a still unusual (for women) profession. In doing so, he demonstrated to a sceptical society that God is not necessarily bad for women. The character bought beer as well as communion bread at the local supermarket, had fun – hosting a "bad taste" 70s party at home – and even applied lipstick before a service!

Which brings me on to another Christian minefield, where some women feel uncomfortable: being "normal". After my conversion, I was a bit of a misfit among Christians. Tempted to church by a group of friends at school – and using the

Jewish Youth Club as "cover" for my parents, who would have been appalled at the very idea I was going to church – I discovered that Jesus was the fulfilment, not the negation, of my Jewish background. God the Father had chosen us as a people, but He had seemed distant. Jesus was utterly accessible, a tangible reflection of God, the Messiah. It all made sense. But not to my parents or friends. Ostracised from the Jewish circle, it was imperative I find acceptance in my new community.

I tried to conform to evangelical expectations, but found it difficult. My fellow-Christians would say "Oh, you're free from the Law now," and then dump a whole load of evangelical dos and don'ts on me that were a lot worse! I was a bit of a rebel. My skirts barely covered my rear, and I wore eye make-up like Dusty Springfield. My mother used to buy my clothes, but what was glitzy for Bar Mitzvahs and discos didn't look right at the CU. I remember turning up once in a red dress with big white circles over the boobs which drew the eye straight to them. I got a reputation for being fast, and Christian boys were terrified of me!

Being assertive is hard for women – and nowhere more than Christian women when it comes to exploring their sexuality. I feel part of my calling is to enable women to feel comfortable with their femaleness. I want to say to Christian women, "Dress to kill!" Yes, we've got to be careful about arousing men, but I'm sure God doesn't mean us to be dull and bland. What Paul was saying, in the famous passage (1 Tim. 2:9), is "Don't make adornment the be-all and end-all."

We are so frightened of porn, that we back off erotica. Yet a survey showed that 30 per cent of women in the US, never mind the UK, are deeply dissatisfied with their sex lives. It's not talked about in church, which says everything: yet in

Judaism, women are entitled to sexual pleasure. It's taught in marriage preparation: a rabbi will explain this to a husband-to-be. Women need help to spice up their sex lives. Maybe a woman needs to take on this area within the church.

Nellie Thornton, the founder of Fashion Services, pioneered the area of fashion for the disabled. Perhaps only a woman could have done that – been aware of the importance of body image in a world exploiting the basic biological instincts of men. Only a woman can understand the pain of not fulfilling the accepted norms of sexual attractiveness. "Yes", said Nellie when I met her, "God is good for women, of every shape, size and age, not just the Linda Evangelistas and Helena Christensens of this world, with their perfect youthful faces and bodies." It was the basic injustice of this that kept Nellie going with her calling, demonstrating to women, and men too, the goodness of a God who loves us exactly as we are.

God can use women in exactly the same way as men. Anything a man can do in the church, in order to serve, is open to us, but we need to see ourselves as full partners with men, in secular as well as Christian work. We put church work on a pedestal, but to be called to be a leader in the secular world is just as important.

Ruth Clark, who became one of the first women Police Superintendents in the country, feels her femininity was vital in her job. "I know I was downgraded because I was seen in tears after dealing with certain cases," she told me. "But it didn't matter. There was a point to be made, that policemen and women are human beings too, that we are affected by what we see and hear."

And God was definitely good for a woman working with criminals: "My faith prevented me from disillusionment with humanity. What was I seeing that the Bible hadn't led me to expect?" And, in rising to the top of her profession, Ruth used her God-given assertiveness without being unfeminine. She proved that a woman could earn respect in a very male world, by being herself and therefore making it more human.

I want to encourage women to use the best that there is in Jewish and Christian tradition, and in the scriptures that they share, to show the world that God is good for us, even if the religious institutions that bear His name are sometimes not. Many outstanding Christian women I have talked to believe God is good for women. They are not always so sure about religious institutions. But whatever is man-made can be changed. If God is good for women, women will be good for the faith.

Girls, what are we waiting for?

*This chapter was written by journalist Alison Burnett,
after an interview with Michele Guinness.*

CHAPTER SEVEN

How to Enjoy the Rest of Your Life

Liz Hansford

Biography

Liz Hansford – just hanging on to her forties by the skin of her teeth – is convinced that the best is yet to be! She is the author of *Not a Super-Saint*, the comic diary of a minister's wife, similar in style to the Adrian Plass diaries – and just as funny! She also writes for a number of Christian magazines and regularly contributes to *Thought for the Day* for Radio Ulster and *Pause for Thought* on Radio 2. Liz has an increasing speaking ministry and also teaches English.

She is married to John, a Baptist pastor, and has four children. She became a mother-in-law for the first time this year!

"The Financial Times Happiness Index indicates that happiness levels have been falling since the 1950s, despite increasing levels of affluence. Happiness, nationally, is at an all time low." Thus ran a spoof, but true, report on the state of the nation's happiness in a recent Radio 4 programme. Officially, we are on a downward route when it comes to joy. But what do you do as a Christian when happiness disappears and your joy gets lost, when all you taste is cardboard and chalk, not the sweetness of God? Is there an alternative to trying harder and buying more? How do you handle disillusionment and mediocrity? How do you cope when you look back at your life and think, "Where did it all go to?", then you look at your waistline and think, "Where did it all come from?" I'm not who I wanted to be and I'm not where I imagined I'd be.

Sometimes behind Christian smiles there's pain and hurt and regret and confusion. And it seems like nothing's quite working out the way we expected. Those secret, inner cries of our hearts need to be heard and answered.

"I'm a pillar of my church, respected and busy. But inside I'm lost spiritually. I do the right things but I don't feel much."

"I waited for the man of God's choice, but he never came. Seems like he never will now. I feel disappointed."

"I got pregnant and ended up marrying the wrong man. I don't think I ever did what God intended me to do."

"I've been married for 23 years and I've four children. I did some calculations recently: I've been on 1,794 grocery shopping trips, hoovered 11,960 rooms, changed 13,140 nappies, cooked 16,790 meals and ironed 71,760 items of clothing. I'm tired."

Add to that the additional burden of Christian expectation and commitment and it isn't surprising to find droves of women short-changed on joy. We think, "Have I achieved anything in life?" "Am I of any significance?" or "Why am I so tired all the time? I don't even have the energy to think about whether I'm happy or not!"

We're disillusioned too. Single ones who wanted to be married. Married ones who wish they'd stayed single. Childless ones who wanted children. Overweight ones who wanted to be slim. Circumstances just aren't the way we'd like them to be. "God is good," we tell ourselves. But at times it doesn't feel like it. So ultimately we've got to face the fact that either there's little joy to be had in God or we're not allowing ourselves to experience it. How do you start to sort such feelings out? You know God promised things like joy and rest, trust and delight, but where are they? Pretending to be happy is not much of an option when you could experience the real thing.

Whenever you find no joy in the Christian life, the very heart of the problem lies in wrong thinking about God and our relationship with him. And since our happiness is based on *who* God is, the best place to start on this search for joy is with what's true about Him and us.

You are God's loved daughter

Number one in the important facts to hold on to when you feel miserable is that you're God's loved daughter and that is not an earned position. The basis for our happiness and security is that relationship, not our performance. God enjoys me. He enjoys you. We don't have to prove anything. There is a secure, loving relationship there already so we can relax. A friend told me recently that he'd been blessed when filling in his tax form. Now my idea of God's blessing is not the Inland Revenue, but I'm keeping an open mind. A rebate, maybe – but the form? "Yes," he said, "it was the bit about dependant relatives. I suddenly realised that as far as God was concerned I was His dependant relative – his child." As his children, naturally we want to please Him. But it is in the context of His total, unconditional acceptance of us. We can do nothing to make him love us more and we can do nothing to make Him love us less.

If we have the idea that He is measuring our pitiful performance against His infinite expectations then we will manufacture for ourselves a faith of rules and works and obedience, where the onus is always on us. We will be weighed down by burdens and duty and anxiety. And if we've been doing that it's no wonder we're so tired and joyless; so much hangs on us. God wants to release us into relationship, not bind us with rules.

Expect more of God

The second truth to hold on to is that God doesn't deal in a watered down version of happiness, a tame version of living that offers only modest pleasures. C.S. Lewis said in his sermon, "Weight of Glory", that we are " like an ignorant child who wants to go on making mud pies in a slum because he cannot imagine what is meant by the offer of a holiday at the sea. We are far too easily pleased." There is more joy than you ever imagined. Don't settle for less than God wants to give you. The trouble is we have been told so often to make the mud pies of sacrifice and duty that we have been deluded into thinking that joy is an unrealistic dream. Remember, God actually commands us to find joy: "Delight yourself in the Lord and he will give you the desires of your heart" (Ps. 37:4). We can't begin to imagine what God has in store for us.

Look in the right place

The third thing to hold on to is that Christianity was made to work in all circumstances. It isn't a faith that depends on nice things happening. So often we focus on what's immediately around us, hoping to find joy there. We try relationships, buying new things, happy events. And these are all fine – until we expect to find lifetime happiness in them. We're like the woman who bought a parrot. She put it in a beautiful cage but it seemed to be unhappy, so she bought it a swing to play on. Still it was no better – in fact the parrot was really failing. So she went on day after day buying it new toys: a mirror, a bell, a ladder – trying desperately to make it happy. But the parrot got sicker and sicker until eventually one day it dropped down from its perch and died. With its final breath it squawked out these words, "Don't they sell any food in that pet shop?" Sometimes we try to fill the emptiness gap with toys. We don't start with what's essential for happiness: God himself. Job 22:25 says: "The Almighty will be your gold ..." And Psalm 16:11 says, "In your presence is fullness of joy. In your right hand there are pleasures for ever." We need to start our search for joy with Him.

But part of the problem is that we don't want to risk all on

God. What if He doesn't deliver? What if He chooses a hard path for me? We think about how things have gone wrong in the past and we don't want to hope too much for the future.

What shape is God's love?

Past experience can tie us down spiritually, and disappointment with life is a serious joy killer. It sets in when life didn't happen as you would have chosen. Perhaps you didn't get to follow the career path you really wanted, you're single and wanted to be married, you're childless and you desperately wanted children, you are battling with a serious illness, you are not financially secure. Essentially the question you ask is, "Does God know best?" "Did He have a plan for me?" "If He didn't give me the things I really wanted, does He love me?" You may become so obsessed with getting what you think will make you happy that that thing becomes the total focus of your life. You beg God to give it to you. And the words written across your life are pain, rejection and loss. You think, "Why me?" God could have made it different and He didn't, so He mustn't really love me.

If you're a *one thing* person you need to ask, "What do I really need to be happy?" Because I can guarantee you, that one thing will never make you truly happy. It may be a legitimate and normal desire, and your heart may feel like it's breaking because you want it so badly. But it may not be what a loving Father has in mind for you. We need to learn to trust, even when circumstances seem negative.

A missionary visiting Tobago was leading worship at a leper colony. When he asked if anyone had a request, a woman who had been facing the back turned around. She had the most hideous face; her nose, ears and lips were entirely gone. She lifted a fingerless hand in the air and asked, "Can we sing, 'Count Your Many Blessings?'" The missionary, overcome with emotion, left the service. A team member followed him and said, "I don't imagine you'll ever be able to sing that song again." "Yes I will," he said, "but I'll never sing it the same way." Look at what God has given you. From a certain perspective your life may look ravaged, but God has blessed you and will bless you. His love doesn't always come in the shape you want. Just open your heart and your arms to Him. Ultimately you need nothing but His love.

To find contentment and joy we need to move from our life plan to the Father's life plan for us. Remember Psalm 84:11: "No good thing does he withhold from those whose walk is blameless." Remember how individual you are. How special. God knows what you need. If you keep your hands closed and only open them for the one gift you want, your closed hands will miss what He so wants to give you.

Is failure forgivable?

Regret too can paralyse us in relation to enjoying life. Regret is when YOU made a bad choice and you live in the shadow of it. Maybe you married the wrong man, perhaps you got pregnant and had an abortion or you ignored God's call on your life. You made the mistake and you live with the consequences. You can't forgive yourself, and in your deepest being you don't really think God could possibly have forgiven you. You wish, how you wish, you could undo the past but you can't. And so your life is characterised by feelings of guilt and what you think is irredeemable failure. In the back of your mind is the thought that one day you might just get this kind of letter from God:

Dear Mrs Brown,

Thank you for your recent application for a place in heaven. We note that your day-to-day contact with senior management has been insufficient, except in moments of dire need. Furthermore, in the area of decision making you have shown a distinct tendency to go your own way and reject instructions given. This has led to disruption of the management's plans for you. Since we have a strong team and family ethos, we feel your actions have been detrimental to the company, its shareholders and, not least, to yourself.

Therefore we regretfully inform you that because of your past life you no longer qualify for such a position.

Yours sincerely,
God

If you're living with major regret, you may worry that that kind of letter will be delivered to your door some morning. You have little joy now because of the past. You think you have left it behind, and then someone says something and it's all triggered off again. If you think like that you are crippled by the past and you haven't really understood the nature of grace and forgiveness. Grace is TOTAL forgiveness for TOTAL failure. It is wipe-out time for sin, all sin. Romans 5:20 says, "Where sin increased, grace increased all the more." It means that that huge sin can have no bearing on your life now. It is covered. Even if it was some often-repeated sin, if it has been confessed and repented of, God's grace has covered it. Nehemiah 9:28 says, "And when they cried out to you again, you heard from heaven, and in your compassion you delivered them TIME AFTER TIME."

Mary Bird was born with a cleft palate. When she started school her classmates made it clear just how they felt about her. To them she was a little girl with a misshapen lip, crooked nose, lopsided teeth and garbled speech. Annually the children had a hearing test in which each child stood by the door and listened while the teacher whispered something which the child had to repeat back to her. It was usually something like "Do you have new shoes?" Mary says, "I waited there for those words that God must have put into her mouth, those seven words that changed my life." The teacher whispered to her, "I wish you were my little girl." Your Heavenly Father says to every woman deformed or handicapped by sin, with a past they wish had never happened, not only, "I wish you were my little girl," but, "You are my little girl." You are accepted and forgiven. That kind of truth, deeply understood and accepted, brings joy. You can enjoy your life when you know your past is a redeemed and forgiven past.

Leave the past behind

The single most important step to take in finding joy in the rest of your life is to leave all those negative past experiences behind you. Leave regret and disappointment, injustice and pain behind and make a conscious decision to move into your future and enjoy God now. In Isaiah 43 God reminds the people of Israel of what He had done in the past for them: He had opened a way through the Red Sea and set them free. But despite even a blessed past, they were to move on in their thinking and *forget the past.*

> *Forget the former things;*
> *Do not dwell on the past.*
> *See, I am doing a new thing!*

92

Now it springs up; do you not perceive it?
I am making a way in the desert
And streams in the wasteland.

(Isa. 43:18,19)

In these verses they were given three basic helps towards a joyful future. First, God was making a way ahead for them in the desert. If you've ever struggled up sand dunes with your shoes full of sand you realise it's not the best path-making territory, but that's the kind of impossible place where God makes a path for you – right into your future. Second, God is out ahead leading, so you'd better look in that direction. Looking backwards in your Christian life is like downhill skiing looking backwards – downright dangerous! You can make real progress when you're focused on the future rather then the past. Third, God has a new thing up ahead for you. Even if you've wasted forty years in the wilderness, just like the Israelites did, it's no limitation on your future. There's still something new for you.

Live with excited anticipation

God clearly expects us to live in hope. Romans 4:18 in *The Message* reads: "When everything was hopeless, Abraham believed anyway, deciding to live not on the basis of what he saw he couldn't do, but on what God said he would do. Abraham didn't focus on his own impotence and say, 'It's hopeless. This hundred-year-old body could never have a child.'" The problem with Abraham was age. It seemed too late to have hope. The simple truth is if it wasn't too late for Abraham it's not too late for you! Age is not a problem with God. Oswald Chambers says, "When we are rightly related to God, life is full of joyful uncertainty and expectancy – we do

93

not know what God is going to do next; He packs our lives with surprises all the time." Whatever your age you should be standing on tiptoe to see what God is going to do next. That kind of tiptoe expectation makes life full of enjoyment.

Start listening

The next clue to finding joy is to start listening to God. You may think you know God's truth. You know it like you know your husband, you've got him sussed after all these years. There isn't anything new he could say to you. When he starts a sentence you could finish it for him – and you sometimes do! You know what he's going to say so much that sometimes you don't stop to listen to what he actually is saying. Have you got God sussed in the same way? You don't expect Him to say anything new to you. He's said it all before. I mean truth is truth – right, and it doesn't change – right. So, God won't say anything new to me. Wrong, He says new things and sets new tasks for open people. And if Bible reading seems dull, or if you've drifted away from it altogether, why not leave the study notes behind and just read until something strikes you – that's God speaking to you, that's the Holy Spirit making the word real! Listen and enjoy it – it wasn't meant to be a guilt trip.

The next thing to do is to get to know yourself. Find out what your spiritual gifts are and start using them. Read the passages to do with spiritual gifts: Romans 12 and 1 Corinthians 12. For too long women have made the tea and looked after the children. And if those are your gifts that's great, but perhaps you have a gift of prayer or of faith. Maybe you have the gift of teaching or administration or counselling. Find out now and start using those gifts. Don't leave it till later and don't worry about what others will say. You have only an audience of one to please. Don't live in conformity. Be who God made YOU to be!

If you want to experience real joy, long term, don't go creating any more regrets. Sheila Miller learned that lesson while serving as a missionary with Overseas Missionary Fellowship in Chefoo. She was on holiday and was so taken up with crochet that her Bible lay closed on the bedroom desk. As she says in her book *I Can Trace a Rainbow* (OMF, 1987), "One of my aids to help me take right decisions is to project myself a few weeks hence. 'Would you prefer,' I asked myself, 'at the end of the holiday, a new crochet jacket or one in-the-making plus hours of fellowship with God.' I was in no doubt. At the end of the holiday, I would have wished I had spent more time with Him." That's an invaluable principle. Project ahead – a week, a month, a year, a lifetime – what will you wish you had done now? Don't settle for a second-rate Christian existence. Don't make choices you'll regret. It's not too late!

It is possible to have a deeper, more joy-giving relationship than you've ever had with God. Open your life for His Spirit to work. Ask Him to fill you to the brim with Himself in a way you've never known before, turn from the past and look forward, so you can fully enjoy the rest of your life.

CHAPTER EIGHT

PRACTISING GOD'S HOSPITALITY

Reona Joly

Biography

Reona Joly-Peterson is a New Zealander by birth and a teacher by profession.

Coming to Europe initially for nine months of study in 1970, the nine months stretched into almost thirty years of involvement as a staff member with Youth With A Mission, based at first in Switzerland and for the past 12 years in England.

While in Lausanne, she met and married Albert, the Swiss administrator of the base there, and their son Pierre was born in 1981.

As a result of a pioneering visit to Albania in 1973, her book *Tomorrow You Die* was published in the mid 1970s and has since been reprinted with an additional chapter updating events in Albania since the Stalinist government was deposed there in 1991.

In addition to being a wife and a mother, Reona travels extensively, teaching on a wide range of subjects relating to Christian life and practice.

What sort of house do you live in?

If I posed this question to a group of women, what interesting and varied answers I would receive: a detached house in the country, a bungalow on the outskirts of a small town, a flat in a tower block in the inner city, a semi-detached, a terrace house, a houseboat on a canal – some would want to describe its age, its size, the materials used in construction, and so on and so on.

In John 1, beginning at verse 35, we have the account of two young men who were being discipled by John the Baptist. As Jesus passed by, John said for the second time, "Look, the Lamb of God!" The curiosity of the young men was aroused and they followed Jesus. Aware that He was being followed, Jesus turned back to them and said, "What do you want?" Their reply was "Teacher, where are you staying?" Jesus did not attempt to give an address, or describe in any way the house where He was staying – instead He issued an open invitation, "Come, and you will see." The young men wasted no time in doing just that. They spent several hours with Jesus and then Andrew went to get his brother Simon. "We have found the Messiah," is what he said. His Christ-centred testimony was so infectious he was able to bring Simon to Jesus. Looking at him Jesus said, "You are Simon son of John. You will be called Cephas."

The story is a familiar one; isn't it interesting that the young men did not ask, "Master, in which synagogue do you worship?" but rather, "Master, where do you live?"

It is extremely rare for our contemporaries to ask us which church we go to, yet so often as part of our witness we feel we ought to take people to our church. But if we have the life of Jesus in us, because folk are curious they wonder what makes us "tick", and Jesus gives us the example: we need to invite people first to our homes, to come close to us, the real us. How many of us live in a "come and see house"?

Are we afraid to bring people close? Are we afraid of the questions they might ask? What if we don't know the answers? Have we said, "There's nothing different in my house to theirs." The attitude does exist in our country of "But my home is my castle", meaning it's for us to enjoy, not others. Are we waiting till the children leave home, or till we can redecorate, till we have more time? The reasons and excuses for not following Jesus' example are numerous, but we have to take seriously the clear command of scripture in Romans 12:13: "Practice hospitality."

It is not really relevant whether the sort of house we live in is large or small, humble or grandiose, immaculate or somewhat untidy or whether, like Jesus, our accommodation is only a borrowed room – what is important is that we who call ourselves Christians have experienced the love that God has for us and we are allowing the love of God to flow through us. Chapter 4, verse 16 of 1 John expresses it perfectly: "And so we know and rely on the love God has for us. God is love. Whoever lives in love lives in God, and God in him."

Chapter 13 of 1 Corinthians describes what God's love is like – it is patient, it is kind, it is free to forgive (it keeps no record of wrongs), it protects, it always trusts, it always hopes, it always perseveres, it never fails. When we are secure in our relationship with Christ, when we know we have been accepted in the Beloved then we can afford to accept other people as they are and to love them with Christ's love. They don't threaten us – we don't need to impress them. We don't need to change them.

In his book, *Reaching Out*, Henri Nouwen shares that "the giving of hospitality is one of the richest biblical terms that can deepen and broaden our insight into our relationships to our fellow human beings. Both Old and New Testament stories show how serious our obligation is to welcome the stranger into our home but they also tell us that guests often carry precious gifts with them which they will reveal to a receptive host."

Abraham received three strangers at Mamre and offered them water, bread and meat. They revealed themselves to him as the Lord and announced that Sarah, his wife, would give birth to a son (Gen. 18:1–15). When the widow of Zarephath offered food and shelter to Elijah, he revealed himself as a man of God offering her an abundance of oil and meal and raising her son from the dead (1 Kings 17:9–24). When the two travellers to Emmaus invited the stranger who had joined them on the road to stay with them for the night, He made Himself known in the breaking of bread as their Lord and Saviour (Luke 24:13–35).

Thus the Biblical stories help us to realise not just that hospitality is an important virtue, but even more that in the context of hospitality, guest and host can reveal their most precious gifts and bring new life to each other.

What are some relevant points to bear in mind when considering hospitality?

- Share what you have and not what you don't have. Don't apologise about the food or the room offered.

- Share what you are and not just what you have. After all beds and meals are provided by hotels. After the meal and the decor are forgotten, people will remember you – the meaningful conversations, the laughter, the atmosphere of love you created.

- Remember your family comes first. It's hypocritical to be gracious to guests but grumpy to husband and children. Learn to simplify things, then you will be more relaxed and pleasant while you prepare.

- The rewards of hospitality are greater than the cost. There are price tags involved in opening our homes – time, energy, food, wear and tear on furniture, and so on. But the rewards are greater. Hospitality enriches marriage and family life. Good friendships between two people are made richer and deeper by exposure to others. Hospitality provides a focus for our homes other than selfishness.

Many of us are good at welcoming Christian friends into our homes, but what about the stranger, the casual acquaintance who is not a church-goer, the neighbour? Galatians 6:10 exhorts us that "as we have opportunity, let us do good to *all* people ..."

Three areas to consider are the difference Christ makes in our attitudes, in our words and in our actions.

We are told by the apostle Paul in Philippians 2, verse 5, that our "attitude should be the same as that of Christ Jesus: Who, being in very nature God ... made himself nothing, taking the very nature of a servant ..." The Christian call – which is the highest possible call – is to serve – with rewards on earth now as well as later in heaven. The world recognises the power that seeks to rule. Jesus and his followers exercise a power that seeks to serve – a power that is mistaken for weakness by the world. Do we see our education, training, social skills, position, possessions and money as qualifying us to rule as the world does, or as having been given in order to serve as Christ did and does?

Our attitudes greatly influence our lives; attitudes are a secret power working twenty-four hours a day, for good or bad. People are not hesitant to ask of us today, "What do you think?" "What do you believe?" "What is your attitude to ... ?" "Do you believe in absolutes, what do you feel about situational ethics?" Sooner or later our environment becomes the result of our inner attitudes. We build our outer world out of our inner.

And what about our words – our speech? There are those who declare themselves to be "silent witnesses". "If we live the Christian life," they say, "people will see Christ in us." But silent witnessing isn't enough. Jesus lived the life perfectly but He also taught continuously. Living the Christian life is difficult. You have to be better, love better and know more than anyone else, for anyone even to notice.

Non-Christians need to hear sincere expressions from the heart of what God means to us and how He makes a difference in our lives. Matthew 12:34 tells us that "out of the overflow of the heart the mouth speaks."

The world is quick to detect words that are insincere, untruthful, manipulative – but the truth spoken in love ministers life, hope and healing: "The mouth of the righteous is a fountain of life"; "The lips of the righteous nourish many"; "The tongue of the wise brings healing" (Prov. 10:11, 21; 12:18). This means as we speak from the overflow of the heart we will share the painful as well as the precious – not just the blessings of the Lord but also His dealings which have brought release, cleansing and restoration.

Paul, speaking to the church in Colossians 4:5,6 (NASB), says: "Conduct yourselves with wisdom toward outsiders, making the most of the opportunity. Let your speech always be with grace, seasoned, as it were, with salt, so that you may know how you should respond to each person." We need to show non-Christians that we care.

"Actions speak louder than words" is a much-used English proverb. The test of spiritual maturity is not our ability to expound or memorise scripture, to exercise many of the spiritual gifts outlined in the New Testament, but it is the willingness to serve God and others through good works – learning to love the unlovely and serve them and to value those whom the world has wounded, abused, discarded.

A true servant of Christ serves inside and outside of the church. The ideal servant sees or hears what needs to be done and does it. Jesus said, "Let your light shine before men, that they may see your good deeds and praise your Father in heaven" (Matt. 5:16). So our good works, inspired and directed by the Holy Spirit, must not be confined within the walls of the church. It has been rightly said that we are to be light because of the darkness of the world.

The New Testament exhorts us to be rich in good works, to be generous and ready to share. It declares that we are His workmanship, created in Christ Jesus for good works. That we are not to love merely with words or tongue but with actions and in truth. We are to be a people of good works. Besides the tongue in our mouth, we have two other tongues, the ones in our shoes. Our lives are epistles, known and read of all men. But the Old Testament is not silent on the subject either. Psalm 37:3 says, "Trust in the Lord, and do good; dwell in the land, and enjoy safe pasture." To trust in the Lord, is that which cannot be seen. But to do good, is the measuring rod. Those who by faith have been made righteous are to demonstrate God's grace in their lives by good works. Can anything be clearer than James' pithy statement: "Faith without deeds is dead!" (2:26).

Mother Teresa, founder of the Missionaries of Charity in Calcutta, commented once on Matthew 25:34–36: "I was hungry and you gave me something to eat." And today Jesus adds, "I am hungry not only for bread, but for love and understanding." "I was a stranger and you invited me in." And today Jesus adds, "I don't suffer just from a lack of shelter; I suffer the homelessness of being unwanted, abandoned, uncared for and unloved." "I needed clothes and you clothed me." And today Jesus adds, "I need more than just a piece of cloth to cover me; I need the covering of human dignity, respect and justice."

The rejected and neglected of our world have every reason to feel more often than not that:

I was hungry and you formed a committee to investigate my hunger;
I was homeless and you filed a report on the indigent;
I was sick and you held a seminar on the under-privileged;
You have investigated all aspects of my plight and I'm still hungry, homeless and sick.

God anointed Jesus of Nazareth with the Holy Spirit and power "... he went about doing good ..." (Acts 10:38).

A lovely story is told of a noble youth in Rome who discovered the riches of God's grace in Christ and gave himself to the Lord who saved him. He went to Hermas, the church leader, with this desire: "What," said he, "can I do in return for such love as this?" Hermas took the high-born young man out into the city of Rome and showed him something of its sin, pointing here and there to the deep spiritual need of its people. Then he said, "Here you will find an altar, here you can become a sacrifice."

In our cities, in our towns and in our rural communities there is unlimited opportunity for us to be involved and to declare that "love listens" (Ps. 81:8, 11, 13); "love learns" (Matt. 11:29); "love leans" (Prov. 3:5).

It is true that we cannot touch our neighbour's heart with anything less than our own. For too long evangelism to many Christians has meant bringing folk to special meetings, or standing on a soap box and delivering a mini-sermon. While handing out tracts on a street corner or maybe knocking on doors and explaining the gospel of Christ, the wisdom and wonder of friendship evangelism has not been grasped. In the *Church Times* of August 1996 the following statement appeared: "Friendship evangelism involves believers befriending non-believers so that the latter may come to see that Christians are different and want to find out about their faith. Friendship evangelists, in other words, spend less time at church meetings and more time at the badminton club or in the pub."

Count Zinzendorf, a German aristocrat, born in the seventeenth century, opened his estate to persecuted evangelicals of Europe. The church faced a critical hour. Luther, Calvin, Huss and Zwingli were sacred memories. Controversy and strife reigned over unimportant matters. The life of Protestantism was being consumed in endless theological strife.

Zinzendorf turned to God in prayer – others joined him. It was on August 14, 1714, as they partook of the bread and wine in a communion service, that the Son of Righteousness arose with healing in His wings. The glory was more than flesh could bear. Believers were prostrate in God's presence. The Cross in all its vast significance was unveiled. The so-called Moravian movement was born. In less than twenty-five years one hundred missionaries had gone out to all parts of the globe. But Zinzendorf was not only concerned with the "uttermost parts of the world". One of his famous statements is, "Let the people see what sort of men and women you are and then they will be forced to ask this question, 'Who makes such men and women as these?'"

In conclusion the amplified version of 1 Peter 4:9 underlies the imperativeness of living in a "come and see house":

Practise hospitality to one another – that is, those of the household of faith. (Be hospitable, be a lover of strangers, with brotherly affection for the unknown guests, the foreigners, the poor and all others who come your way who are of Christ's body). And (in each instance) do it ungrudgingly (cordially and graciously, without complaining but as representing Him).

(Amp. Bible)

CHAPTER NINE

Using Our Hands

Priscilla Reid

———— ⚵ ————

Biography

Priscilla Reid is on the leadership team of both the Lifelink team, a group of churches in Ireland committed to church planting and resourcing other churches, and also the Christian Fellowship Church, Belfast.

Priscilla is a frequent speaker at Spring Harvest and other major conferences. She has a strong prophetic gifting and longs to see Ireland and the nations reached with the Good News of the Gospel.

In her spare time she looks after four daughters and her husband Paul!

When God speaks to you in the middle of a wonderful conference, with inspired worship and heart-stirring messages, it is all too easy to respond with undiluted enthusiasm. However, in the cold light of day you can talk yourself out of it very easily, putting it all down to the indigestible frozen pizza you had hurriedly grabbed at teatime. It happened to me recently, when I felt the Lord challenge me during a conference we hosted at the church I am part of in Belfast. "Take what you have experienced here and share it with women in India," the Lord said very clearly.

It wasn't totally "out-of-the-blue", I had visited India once before and over many years our church had sent teams out to Andra Pradesh to work in partnership with a network of churches there. Nevertheless, when I come back down to earth after the conference, the thought of taking a team to India filled me with apprehension. What did I have to offer women from a country and culture about which I knew so little? How would I connect with them, when their way of life was so vastly different? Then there was the language barrier.

I was back-peddling as hard and fast as I could, when I met a woman in England who had visited India several times and she said that God had asked her, "What do you have in your hand?" as He had asked Moses thousands of years ago. The question reverberated in my mind and heart days after our conversation and eventually I said, "I have so little Lord, just a love for these women whom I have only met once before but who found a place in my heart", and I found the Lord assuring me that that was enough.

We are living in momentous days, when God is moving in incredible ways around the world. The great advantage of this media age is that we can hear so easily what is going on in the far-flung regions of the earth. God is mobilising women of all ages, in many different countries, and using them alongside men to build His church and bring in His Kingdom. These are days to face our insecurities and allow God to help us overcome them in order to take our place and play our part in this vast army. One of our strengths as women is that we can see our weaknesses and admit to them, but the disadvantage of this is that we often allow those weaknesses to disqualify us. Someone has said that a man looks at a job and sees the 75 per cent he can do but a women looks at the 25 per cent she can't do and counts herself out.

A few years ago our local folk museum telephoned me and asked if I would be interested in doing storytelling sessions for them. Before I had the children, I was a librarian and regularly held such sessions, but I hadn't "worked" for sixteen years and so began to make excuses over the phone. My husband Paul was jumping up and down behind me with frustration, "Say yes, you've told the children more stories in the last sixteen years than you've made them hot dinners!" I don't know if that was a comment on my culinary expertise but I did realise how ridiculous I was being in turning down the opportunity, so I did a quick U-turn and agreed.

God wants us to take a long look at our hands, asking us to respond to the question, "What is in your hand?" It is even worth taking a few minutes to sit and physically hold your hands out in front of you and give yourself a chance to answer the question. Few of us would be able to list the accomplishments of the woman in Proverbs 31 who "works with eager hands". She had so much in her hands it is intimidating: she was a business woman, a manufacturer, a farmer, a property developer, a creative person, the list goes on and on. Sometimes, if I'm being honest, I think if I knew her I wouldn't like her!

My reaction isn't far removed from our attitude to gifted people we meet in real life – because they intimidate us, we attack and reject them. God has given us a profile of this woman not to intimidate us but to inspire us. Somehow we think it is vaguely unspiritual to admit that we have something to offer. The old hymn comes to mind, "Nothing in my hand I bring, simply to thy cross I cling", and this is entirely true when it comes to our salvation. It is a free gift and we do nothing to earn it but, as his children, God wants us to be able to recognise that there is something in our hands that we can give back to Him.

Did you ever sing the nursery song with a toddler, "Tommy Thumb, Tommy Thumb, where are you?" The rhyme goes through each of the child's fingers in turn and they pop them up with, "Here I am, here I am, how do you do?" When it came to thinking what I had in my hand, I imagined the Lord was encouraging me to see myself sitting on my heavenly Father's knee, enjoying the companionship and security of looking at my hands together.

If you look at your little finger first, it doesn't seem very significant and that is a reflection very often of how we feel. If I have anything in my hand at all it is pitifully small and unimportant. However, scripture is full of examples of people who gave seemingly insignificant things to God who then multiplied them and produced more than their wildest imaginings. The little boy who brought his lunch of five loaves and two fish to Jesus comes to mind, as does the widow of Zarephath in 1 Kings 17 with "a little flour and a little oil".

Another widow in 2 Kings 4 was in desperate straits, with the creditors coming to take her sons. She replied to Elisha, when he asked her what she had in her house, "Your servant has nothing there at all except a little oil."

Was that your initial reaction when you read the question, "What do you have in your hand?" I have nothing, absolutely nothing but now there is a gentle whisper within you, "except a little ..." I have a little love to give, a little encouragement, a little hospitality, a little creativity, a little gift. If we will open up our hands to God and give him the little we have then, like the widow, we can stand back in amazement at what God can do with it. From that "little oil", God filled every container the widow could lay her hands on and rescued both her sons and herself.

Recently my husband Paul visited Brazil where he met Elizabeth Cornelio who had become a Christian from a spiritist background and now leads a prayer network in the city she lives in of 100,000 intercessors. This is a network that is given prayer requests by the city council and police authority because they recognise the spiritual authority of the people of God and their ability to pray and see situations radically changed. She is part of a long line of women in church history like Catherine Booth, Elizabeth Fry, Corrie Ten Boom and Jackie Pullinger-To, who brought the little they had, gave it to God and let Him multiply it. The more sobering thought is that, according to the parable of the talents in Matthew 25, we need to use what we have, otherwise even the little we have will be taken away from us. The servant in the story was driven by fear of his master and it immobilised him. We are in a love relationship with our heavenly Father and He wants to encourage us to make the most of what He has given to us.

That love relationship is underlined when we look at our hands and see the ring that the Father has given us. When the prodigal son returned to the father's house, along with the kiss, the robe and the sandals he received a ring. The father's ring was a symbol of belonging, a sign of the father's acceptance and love, but it was also a symbol of authority. When officials carried the king's ring, they commanded all the respect and authority of the king himself. In an insecure world, as women of God we need to know who we belong to and that we are deeply loved, and the Father has put a ring on our finger.

We not only experience that love and security for ourselves but God places it in our hands so that we can give it away. This love is not based on how good-looking we are, how slim we are, how intelligent or gifted we are, it is not an acceptance based on externals or conformity to some arbitrary set of values. It is the wonderful reckless grace of God, which embraces us and accepts us just as we are. God always meant us to live in the good of knowing that He loves us, not just an intellectual assent but a knowing, in the depth of our being, that lights up our lives and motivates our actions. It is the love that Paul prays we will experience in Ephesians 3:17–19, "And I pray that you, being rooted and established in love, may have power, together with all the saints, to grasp how wide and long and high and deep is the love of Christ, and to know this love that surpasses knowledge – that you may be filled to the measure of all the fulness of God."

When God speaks your name and tells you that He loves you, as He did for me many years after I became a Christian, it brings a release and joy into your relationship which head knowledge alone can never achieve. If this is an area that you struggle with, look at your ring finger and see the ring the Father has given to you, still your spirit and hear His voice speak of His love for you. Then you will rise up with new confidence and authority and be able to give this unconditional love away to others who live in a society which starves them of acceptance and love unless they conform to its superficial standards.

In the action rhyme the middle finger is "Toby Tall", for obvious reasons, and as we look at what is in our hands, we need to ask ourselves, "What is the biggest thing I have in my hand?" Perhaps a problem, or something you are currently struggling with, comes to mind. You are carrying a burden in your hands and it is all you can see as you look at them. Jesus invites us to bring the burden to Him, so that He can replace it with His peace and then, when we take a fresh look at our hands, we will be able to see that the greatest thing we have in our hands is worship.

The woman who gate-crashed Simon the Pharisee's dinner party for Jesus understood that the most precious thing she had in her hands was not the expensive perfume but the love and adoration of her heart. She was so determined to express her love that she refused to be held back by other people's opinions of her. Simon was horrified that Jesus would allow this sinful woman to touch Him, and she would have been only too well aware of what the people in that house thought of her. Fear of men did not intimidate her but passion for Jesus motivated her. It was an uncontrolled passion which made Simon – and no doubt his friends – highly uncomfortable but, if we are being honest, it would have made most of us react in exactly the same way. The woman cried so profusely that Jesus' feet were wet, she used her hair as a towel to dry them and then she showered His feet with kisses, before pouring the perfume over them.

Often when we read the Gospels our familiarity with the stories sanitises them and strips them of emotion. If we really stop and think of what it would have been like to be in Simon's house that night, the enormity of the woman's actions would overwhelm us. It wasn't enough for her to feel this intense love for Jesus, she had to express it and Jesus obviously appreciated it and commended her actions.

God gave us our emotions, but often in the church today they are viewed with suspicion and undermined as "the flesh". We excuse our lack of expressiveness with reassurances that God knows how we feel about Him in our hearts. I was a Christian for many years before my life was impacted by the power of the Holy Spirit. I loved the Lord, the Spirit of God lived in me but, because of the Christian traditions I had been brought up in, I had never understood the need to open up all of my life to the Spirit of God. When I did, it felt as if someone had taken the key and unlocked my own spirit, setting me free to worship God in a more expressive way. When we began to wave banners and flags as part of our worship I joined in with great enthusiasm. One lady really struggled with the whole idea, feeling it was irreverent and not suitable in a worship service. In a burst of over-excitement I "gently" informed her, "Listen, I don't just want to wave a flag, I want to fly with the flag!"

Jesus contrasted Simon's cold aloofness to the woman's warm-hearted passion and suggested it was because she knew how much she had been forgiven that she acted in the way she did. Self-righteousness and a sense of our own goodness will stifle the expression of our worship, it's when we take a long hard look at ourselves and realise that, without Jesus, we would be ugly because of our sin, that we can run to Him with reckless abandon. As we look at our hands, the greatest thing in them is our worship which we can give to God.

I love the fact that, for many days after this incident, if you had met either Jesus, or the woman, the aroma of the perfume would have remained with them. This was not some cheap watered down imitation, this was top of the range, pure perfume, worth a small fortune, so it wouldn't have faded five minutes after it had been put on like some of the stuff I buy! She was able to give something to the Lord and, in return, the fragrance of her worship remained with her. It reminds me of how Paul describes Christians in 2 Corinthians 2:14, that God "through us spreads everywhere the fragrance of the knowledge of him. For we are to God the aroma of Christ among those who are being saved and those who are perishing. To the one we are the smell of death; to the other, the fragrance of life".

This neatly brings us to our fourth finger in the children's song, "Peter Pointer". What do you have in your hand? You can point people to Jesus. Perhaps your reaction to this is the same as mine, "Not me, I'm not an evangelist." I get so frustrated with people who tell amazing stories of how they get the chance to share Jesus with people they meet on the bus, in the street, at the shops – they even have people knocking at their doors. It's the Christian equivalent of the comedian's opening gambit of, "A funny thing happened to me on the way to the show", which becomes "a wonderful thing happened to me on the way to the meeting".

I thought my choice of having a wonderful story to tell had come several years ago, when I had to fly from Portland, Oregon, home to Belfast, on my own. Every preacher worth their salt has an aeroplane story to tell and so this was my big opportunity. Unfortunately, despite looking reasonably friendly, I managed to fly from Portland to San Francisco to London to Belfast without having a conversation with a single soul!

I have been a Christian for many years and have swung from beating myself up because of not being effective in evangelism, to consoling myself with the thought that it's not my gift and I'll leave it to others who do get their doors battered on. It is only recently that, when I have looked at what I had in my hand in connection with evangelism, I realised my gift was friendship. I can be a friend and often the best way to develop friendship is not as a lone exercise but within the community of the church. We meet one another's friends and in that context – by our lives and our words, when applicable, we can point people to Jesus.

The final digit we need to think about is the thumb, which enables us to grip whatever is in our hand. When we discover what is in our hands, as the Holy Spirit reveals it to us, we can only take hold of it by prayer. No matter what else we hold in our hand, we need to see that without prayer it will be ineffective. Few of us see ourselves as great prayer warriors but it is vitally important that we don't consign prayer to the few intercessors that we know and whom we think of as super-spiritual beings, standing apart from the rest of us. Thank God for the men and women who have given themselves to prayer in the church, but prayer is not a specialist ministry, prayer is for everyone. E.M. Bounds made the point that Satan trembles even when the weakest Christian prays because he knows that "they go to fetch strength against him". When we became Christians, whether we realised it or not at the time, we were launched into a battlefield and, in order to survive, we need to ensure that we put on the armour of Ephesians 6. God has provided the shield of faith for us and this defensive weapon enables us to "extinguish all the flaming arrows of the evil one" (v.16). All the accusation and condemnation he flings at you can find no place to enter your spirit as you defend yourself with the shield of faith. We also need to take up our offensive weapon, the sword of the Spirit, which is the word of God, and learn to wield it as effectively as Jesus did when confronted with the temptations of Satan in the wilderness.

There is a battle on for our families, our children, our friends, our communities and we have the weapons in our hands that can push back the kingdom of darkness and take ground for the kingdom of God. Matthew 11:12 tells us that the kingdom of God is advancing and forceful men and women need to take hold of it. Let's not lie down under Satan's intimidation and threats but rise up as warriors in God's army, taking our place alongside our brothers and sisters in Christ, in order to see the work of Christ on the cross established in the lives of the people we love and live among.

It is vitally important that we begin to believe that as women we have something to offer, but it is not enough to recognise what is in our hands, we need to mix it with faith in order to make it effective. Faith always seems daunting – what if we don't have enough? Jesus said that if we have faith the size of a grain of mustard seed we could say to the mountain to be moved into the sea and it would have to go. If you cut open an apple you can count the number of seeds in it but, as a Dutch friend of mine pointed out to me, it is impossible to count the number of apples in the seed. The next time you hold an apple seed in your hand think of the number of apples it could produce. When we offer what is in our hands to God and mix it with faith the potential for harvest is beyond what we can imagine. Ultimately what we can achieve with what is in our hands is because we are in God's hands, our wonderful heavenly Father who will never let us go.

CHAPTER TEN

WHO ON EARTH AM I?

Jennifer Rees Larcombe

—— ☙ ——

Biography

Jennifer Rees Larcombe is a speaker and Christian counsellor and runs a small healing centre in Kent. She loves introducing people to Jesus. She has had twenty-two books published.

Jennifer spent eight years in a wheelchair and, after thirty apparently happy years of marriage, her husband left her two years ago for someone else. She believes that as God healed her physically after eight years in a wheelchair, He can mend her marriage too. She says that "forgiving isn't easy and rejection hurts like hell, but we can decide to live in bitterness or in God's blessing".

Jennifer spends much of her time with women struggling with disappointing or painful marriages, or with those, like herself, whose marriages have broken down.

She has six children and two grandchildren.

The other day I saw someone waving at me in the street. She seemed to know me, and I knew I *ought* to know her, but ...

"I don't blame you for not recognising me," she said, as I squirmed with embarrassment. "I've put on four stone since last year." All three of her children had left home within a few months and suddenly she was alone. "I've been a mum for twenty-five years, but now I don't know who I am any more," she confessed. "I get so panicky I eat for comfort."

"Who am I and where do I fit in this world?" Most of us never have to time to stop and ask ourselves that question – until life suddenly removes our props and landmarks, and in our bewilderment we are forced to stop and consider our personal identity.

Am I who I belong to?

As a child, I knew exactly where I fitted in the world, I was Tom and Jean Rees's daughter – I belonged to the Rees family. Then, one August day, I changed my identity and became the wife of Tony Larcombe. In an embarrassingly short time we had six children, so I was known in our village as "the woman with all those kids". I was proud to be pointed out as "Justyn's Mum" when he won the cup on Sports Day, but not so pleased to be Duncan's when he kicked his football through our neighbour's window.

Many women are someone else's daughter, wife, mother or PA all their lives and, like the friend I met in the street, are quite content to hide the "real them" behind other people. Yet, because their identity is based on who they belong to, what happens when their elderly parents die, their husband leaves them and the children grow up? They face a massive identity crisis.

Am I what I do?

"I'm a social worker – a doctor – a policewoman."

"I know who I am when I've got my uniform on," a nurse told me once, "but off duty, I don't feel I'm a person." Jobs and professions can certainly give us status and identity, but we can also hide behind our hobbies and interests.

"I'm the captain of the Golf Club – a member of the WI – a horticultural judge – a champion dog breeder." Christian women can find their identity in church work: "I run the Sunday school – lead the worship group – head up the Evangelism Committee."

Of course, wrapping our identity in what we do means we have to succeed, at all costs, to prove we are a valuable person. This puts huge pressure on us because failing is unthinkable. And suppose we retire, become redundant or we are voted off the committee? What if a new minister arrives who abolishes our Sunday school or asks his wife to run the music group? Who are we then?

Am I what I look like?

For many women being beautiful is all important. The size 12 figure, stylish hair and designer clothes are the walls behind which they hide the real person they fear might not be so attractive or impressive as they want others to think they are. Perfection isn't always easy to maintain, remember Princess Diana and her bulimia; and no one can help growing old.

Am I my problem?

Last year I was asked to speak at a conference for people suffering from eating disorders and I got talking to a girl suffering from anorexia. She looked more like a skeleton than a young woman of twenty-three. "I'm afraid if I started eating again I wouldn't know who I am," she told me. "My anorexia gives me an odd kind of reason for living – fighting my family and the medics. I can hide inside the illness, because I guess I'm afraid to face real life." What a remarkably honest person she was! I guess we all know people in our churches who lurch from one problem to the next, almost as if they *have* to be the focus of everyone's attention. Perhaps they fear we'll find the "real them" boring?

I was totally content with my identity as a country housewife and mother of a large brood, when suddenly I became seriously ill and spent the next eight years dependent on a wheelchair. For a long time I struggled madly against being seen as a "disabled person". The last thing I wanted was to be just a hospital "case" or a number on a DSS file. Yet I could no longer look after my family – they had to care for me – and the only way to avoid frustration was to let the old identity go and accept the new one as gracefully as I could.

Am I who you think I am?

If a husband or boss tells a woman often enough she's an incompetent fool, she'll become one! We can also grow up with a picture of ourselves derived from the opinions of our parents or other adults who were important in our childhood.

"You're so clumsy – more like a carthorse than a little girl! Why can't you be graceful like your cousin Ann?" That kind of remark, if repeated often enough, can send a woman out into adult life feeling like a clumsy elephant.

The words "You should have been a boy", were said so often to my friend, Clare, that now she always wears jeans and sweatshirts and cuts her own hair – you can tell she does!

"You're a troublemaker; a walking disaster; thick as a post; accident prone. You take after your Auntie and remember what happened to her!"

It's hardly surprising that someone, spoken to like that in childhood, is most unlikely to think of herself as anything but a failure.

Realising we are not the person everyone believed we were can be a lengthy process because it is hard to break the restrictive mould imposed on us by others.

> I'm not who I think I am.
> I'm not who YOU think I am,
> I am who I think you think I am.

That is a very telling poem, but it doesn't have to be true!

All the ways that we have just discussed of finding our identity are too ephemeral and risky to be relied upon, so how do we find the true way?

How do I discover who I am?

Perhaps our outward identity changes many times throughout a lifetime – which can be most unsettling because change and readjustment are always stressful. So we need to find our true identity which can remain permanent while the "outside us" continues to alter its appearance. Let me tell you how that has worked out for me.

After those eight years of being "a disabled person", with an orange badge and a pension book, I was suddenly healed through prayer. I had to begin a totally new life; new job; new role in the world; new fit, healthy me. Strange to say the adjustment was not without difficulties but I loved having the house filled with teenagers; and developing a Christian ministry with my husband was great fun. I dreaded the last of my six children leaving home, after so many years of motherhood, but I told myself the Darby and Joan days lay ahead to be enjoyed, too. Our thirty years of marriage had always been very happy and fulfilling – for me anyway. However, two weeks after our youngest son went to university my husband told me he had fallen in love with someone else and was leaving to live with her. Yet another new identity was forced on to me – "separated" – "deserted wife". How I hated it!

When I realised my husband really had gone and the shocked numbness began to wear off, I constantly asked myself, "Who on earth am I, and what's the point of it all?' I was no one's daughter or wife, and no longer had children to hide behind; the ministry we had built together looked like toppling, leaving me without a role, and suddenly all the familiar fixtures of my life were gone.

One horrible winter night, a few months after my husband left, I really reached the sludge at the bottom of the "sewer". I had never lived alone in my life, and my bungalow is right out in the sticks. A storm outside produced all kinds of sinister noises which terrified me. My desk was piled with forms I couldn't understand and bills I couldn't pay; the loo had blocked, flooding the bathroom floor and – worst of all – there was a mouse in my bedroom cupboard. In total despair I wrapped myself in a rug and curled up on the sofa.

The terrible sense of abandonment was overwhelming. Everyone was gone. All the voices and laughter a large family generates were silent. A terrible feeling of shame and failure also engulfed me as endless regrets surged into my mind.

"If only I'd been more loving; tinted my hair; shown interest in cricket; gone to Weight Watchers..." Frankly, right then, I wished I were dead! Then suddenly I remembered a card a friend had sent me that morning with a message scrawled inside. "Take a look at Isaiah 54." I hadn't bothered – the last thing I felt like doing was Bible study – but I had to pass the night somehow. When I found the place these words "jumped" out at me:

> *'Do not be afraid; you will not suffer shame ... For your Maker is your husband – the Lord Almighty is his name ... you were a wife deserted and distressed in spirit – a wife who married young, only to be rejected,' says your God ... 'Though the mountains be shaken and the hills be removed, yet my unfailing love for you will not be shaken ...'*

Somehow I felt He was presenting me with a challenge. Was I going to believe His promise, or simply grind on in my own misery?

I knew the ideal Old Testament husband was his wife's protector, provider and spiritual teacher, and from him she derived her status and, of course, her identity. He literally was responsible for her welfare and happiness, to a degree which is hard for us to comprehend. Was God really offering to be there for me to such an extent as that?

I had always thought of Him as my Heavenly Father, my boss and even my friend, but this was a far deeper level of intimacy.

"Surely the symbol only applied to Israel?" I was arguing with my own incredulity. "No, there were all those New Testament references to Christians being the bride of Christ. But wasn't He talking about a collective relationship, applying to a whole nation?" I was still struggling! Then I realised that most of the references to God being a father were addressed to

Israel or the church, yet we always think of Him as our personal Heavenly Father as well.

Gradually it dawned on me that He really was offering me a relationship as intimate as an ideal marriage – when the two merge and become "one flesh" (Gen. 2:24). He was also promising to be responsible for meeting my practical, as well as my emotional, needs. "All right Lord," I whispered. "I've got no one else now, so I'm just going to have to trust you."

Nothing has been the same since. Slowly, one by one, my "husband" helped me sort those direct debits, mortgage repayments, the broken loo and leaking roof – and I don't know what He did about the mouse, but I've never seen it again! The way He has met my financial needs has been quite miraculous, but He has also given me such a sense of being special and deeply loved that the grief and insecurity inside me is healing nicely. Of course, I get lonely sometimes but He always seems to send round just the right person when He knows I need to see His love wrapped in human skin. Most of all, I've realised, more completely than ever, just what He did for me on the cross. All those regrets and "if onlys" have been firmly chucked into the dustbin which stands at its foot.

Now when I see couples walking hand in hand or sitting close together in church, and that old surge of misery engulfs me, I think, "But I'm with my husband, too. I'm holding His hand, even if I can't see it!"

I am sure the exquisite closeness that I am experiencing through this insight is not simply for widows and deserted wives. I guess there are many married women who feel deeply disappointed. Their husbands simply do not meet their practical or emotional needs. Nagging and pleading have no effect so they have to choose between leaving and stepping outside God's covering, or remaining – unfulfilled. We all long for love and appreciation but human relationships so often fail to provide them. I can promise you, from my own experience, that God really can meet *all* our needs when we decide to depend on Him for support in every area of our lives. Who knows, some unhappy marriages might even improve when the wife finds her fulfilment in God, thus taking the pressure off her husband to become something he can probably never become!

I am also sure that single women don't have to be nuns to feel married to God. This lovely relationship is on offer for us all, if we want to accept it. Our Bridegroom says to us; "Arise, my darling, my beautiful one, and come with me. See! The winter is past; the rains are over and gone. Flowers appear on the earth; the season of singing has come" (Song of Songs 2:10–12).

After that remarkable night I stopped asking "who am I?" My identity is no longer wrapped up in anyone, or anything, but Jesus.

I really am who I belong to

When we belong to God and are "in Christ" He says; "Fear not ... I have summoned you by name; you are mine" (Isaiah 43:1).

I am also what I do

Yes, I write books for my "Husband", and speak at events for Him too, but my identity is not vested in any of that. I am called, like everyone else, simply to be a radiator. Not the kind which is fixed to the wall and pumps out heat, but the kind which radiates the warmth of God's love to everyone we encounter. The radiator in my sitting room stores electricity during the night and then uses it to keep me warm next day. As we spend time with Him we are filling ourselves up with

His love, ready to pass it on to others through whatever kind of ministry, role or church position we may have: "Each one should use whatever gift he has received to serve others, faithfully administering God's grace in its various forms" (1 Peter 4:10).

I am not what I look like – on the outside

I'm glad of that, I wouldn't make much of a bride at my age! But then God doesn't look at the outside of us, he looks at our hearts.

It was April, and I was on holiday in the Greek islands when I saw something I will never forget. It was their Easter celebration and the main town of the island was packed for the Good Friday procession. People came from outlying hamlets and farms, wearing their very best clothes, and among them was the most beautiful girl I ever saw. The young man who held her hand looked like a Greek god and it was obvious they were just married. "How quickly a bride's perfection fades," I thought sadly, and I found myself imagining her future visits to the Easter Festival. Next year she might look a big peaky and sick, with the onslaught of her first pregnancy. The following year her hips and stomach might not be quite so trim, and bags could be appearing under her eyes from sleepless nights with a teething baby. A few years on she would have several children pulling at her skirts and a toddler on her hip; her figure would be shapeless and the sun might have wrinkled and coarsened her skin. As the years rolled by her lovely black hair would turn grey, dazzling teeth would disappear and her long legs would be bent and twisted by arthritis. The lovely bride I had so admired would be a dumpy old woman, hobbling up the street, in no time at all.

Yes, I know that sounds depressing, but ageing happens to

us all – on the outside. However, when God takes us on, our bodies may be young, but our spirits are wrinkled and blotched by sin and distorted by the weight of the self-confidence we carry. Bit by bit He begins to change us, using all the adversities and problems of life to draw us towards himself, stripping away our weighty self-dependence, and smoothing our ugly attitudes. He aims to turn us into the radiantly beautiful bride He desires (Ephesians 5:27). What a gloriously romantic prospect, and it certainly takes the sting out of getting old!

I'm not what I think I am

I am not what other people think I am.
I am what HE thinks I am.

One of the most remarkable things that I've ever realised is that when God looks at me, He sees me as pure, innocent and absolutely perfect. I don't see myself like that! Others certainly don't see me like that, but because of what Jesus did for me on the cross God thinks I'm perfect!

He also thinks I'm incredibly valuable. When the man you love best in the world suddenly dumps you, you feel utterly worthless – nothing but rubbish. Yet my "Husband" was prepared to give His life for me. An object is only as valuable as the price someone is prepared to pay for it. A plastic cup holds just as much tea as an antique cup made of porcelain. One is worth a few pence, the other is worth thousands of pounds to a collector. My "Husband" was willing to pay all He had for me, so I must be a VIP – and, of course, so are you!

God doesn't always give us the identity we want to have – the happily married wife, the top executive, the politician, the high-powered preacher. He will, however, make us the person

He wants us to be, if we let Him: "For I know the plans I have for you," declares the LORD, "plans to prosper you and not to harm you, plans to give you hope and a future" (Jeremiah 29:11).

A Good Read: Women in the Gospels of Luke and John

Elaine Storkey

Biography

Elaine Storkey is the Co-President of Tear Fund, Vice President of Cheltenham and Gloucester College, and a member of the General Synod of the Church of England. She is involved in a wide range of other Councils and Trusts. She also has counselling experience and works with a number of people with relational difficulties.

She has lectured widely throughout the world to universities, churches and conferences.

In England she is known to many through her regular BBC broadcasts with Radio 4 and BBC Wales and her appearances on television.

Elaine is also a widely-read author. She has written for the Open University, especially in the area of social analysis. Her main book, *What's Right with Feminism,* has gone through seven printings and awaits a second edition. Another publication, *Mary's Story, Mary's Song,* was the Archbishop of Canterbury's Lent book for 1994, which is being revised and reissued under the new title *Magnify the Lord.* Recently published by Hodder & Stoughton, her latest book, *Search for Intimacy,* explores the structures and barriers to good relationships. She has written many articles for journals and newspapers including the *Guardian* and the *Independent.*

Elaine was born in Wakefield, and is married to Alan Storkey, an economist, writer and lecturer. They have three sons.

We learn one important thing from the shelves of women's magazines and women's novels in the local bookshop: it is that women are interested in the lives of other women. Thousands of pages are devoted to telling the stories of love, relationships, struggles and rejoicings. And women read them. This is more than just being fascinated with gossip. Some psychologists say it is part of a sense of "connectedness" that defines the way many women order their lives. Women have always played an important part in the emotional lives of others. Many of us know ourselves primarily in relationship. We are someone's friend, someone's daughter, mother, sister, wife, neighbour, cousin. So their news interests us. Their details absorb us. Their lives matter to us.

It is not surprising, therefore, that there are so many novels, plays, magazines, short stories that are written for and by women. They engage our minds and feelings by drawing us into the daily aspects of the lives of others. Anyone who wants to reach the hearts of women knows they can do it through story-telling, through sharing things that matter to them and telling it how it is. This is not new. For centuries women have been absorbed in hearing about other women, curious to see how similar or different such lives are from our own. Their stories grip us. Tales of pain or suffering, heroism and achievement, sacrifice and service – we have ears to hear them all.

Christian women are no exception to this. We have loved our stories of missionaries, of pioneers, of women who have broken the mould and risked everything to serve Christ. We have enjoyed girls' novels which travel with imagination and give us cameos of people's intricate lives and their longings for God. We love to narrate the incidents of our own lives to one another, hearing the next episode, turning the next page over.

That is why it is so satisfying when we come across stories of women in the Gospels themselves. For we share their faith; we watch their journey; we hear their heartbeat. Through the snapshots of their lives we get to know them better. Through their encounters with Jesus we get to know Jesus better. What is more, these incidents are not just for women of faith. Women who have little contact with the church or the Scriptures can find in these narratives something which strikes them. The truth of what they read can speak deep into their own lives.

There are many differences between the accounts of the Gospel writers, even in the narratives about women. That should not surprise us, for they were all different people and told their story from different angles. Luke was the only doctor. Matthew was a Jewish Christian, probably a former tax collector. Mark was most likely John Mark, writing down some of the stories from Peter, and John was almost certainly the "disciple whom Jesus loved". They passed on the same tradition, but often glimpsed things that were different from one another. It is one of the amazing things about the Word of God that God has entrusted it to human beings, and allowed them to communicate His eternal truth through their own personalities and background.

Yet for some people it is still a problem that the Gospel writers were men, not women. They want women to have their own voices, to speak for themselves. They fear that with the accounts recorded by men, women's experiences have simply been edited out. Others have spoken in our place and can get us wrong. Yet that is clearly not true. So many of the stories in the Gospels are indeed women's stories. They are insights into the lives and longings of women. Not only are these incidents about women, they sometimes describe situations where only women were present. So although they were written down by men, the narratives must have often have originated from the women themselves. How else did the author know that Mary "pondered all these things in her heart" if Mary herself had not told him. For this was Mary's story. How did the author know the details of the conversation between Jesus and the woman at the well, if the Samaritan woman had not given those details herself? For this was the Samaritan woman's story. How did the author know about the conversation between the women going to the tomb, if the women had not first told the story? For this was the resurrection story communicated by faithful women. The Gospels are not about male authors. They are a community of belief which is held in common. Truth is passed down, and women and men share together in the telling.

Women in Luke's Gospel

Luke is often thought of as the Gospel writer most interested in women. And for good reason. Their lives come tumbling out of the pages of his Gospel as we read their experiences with Jesus. As the "beloved physician" we would expect him to be particularly interested in ailing or sick women. And he is. Dr Luke is the one who tells us of the the woman who suffered from menstrual problems for twelve years, having spent all her money without any relief, and who now risks breaking the taboos against menstruation by joining the crowd around Jesus (Luke 8). Luke tells us of the woman who had been crippled for eighteen years and whose miraculous recovery upsets the leaders of the synagogue (Luke 13). Luke draws us into the tale of Jairus's daughter whose parents are beside themselves with worry, and who is dead by the time we get to her home (Luke 8). Luke even takes us to a funeral procession where a widow's only son is being taken for burial, to the great distress of his mother and her friends (Luke 7). Luke is familiar with women's illnesses and with death. And he knows miraculous healing when he sees it. He lets us know, too, that all of these women find in Jesus someone who meets them where they are. Dread is turned into joy, fear into freedom, anxiety into release.

Yet Luke is interested also in the stories of women who are not sick or suffering. It would seem that he simply has real insight into how women feel and what matters to them. And in that he reflects the insight of Jesus himself. He tells us about Elizabeth and Mary, the two pregnant cousins, separated by age and distance until Mary makes a journey (Luke 1). He tells about the widow who gives her "mite", everything she has, to the offering (Luke 21). He tells about Mary and Martha, those sisters whose idea of hospitality is very different (Luke 10). He tells about the women who follow Jesus great distances, and support Him out of their own income (Luke 8). He tells about how the women go in sorrow to anoint a dead body and find instead an empty tomb (Luke 24).

Luke never hides from us the details of women's lives, nor their part in the worship and praise of God. It is Luke's gospel that contains the Magnificat – the outpouring of rejoicing from the virgin mother to the liberating God – a passage which has gone down through the centuries as a praise song in the church. It is Luke's gospel that recalls Christ's words of gratitude to the woman who lavished perfume on Him and washed His feet with her tears. It is Luke's gospel that reminds us that the glorious message of resurrection was given to women, that Christ is not dead, but is risen. For good reason women have found especial inspiration and encouragement in the writings of Luke right through the centuries.

The story of the resurrection is one of the key stories of all times. It is interesting to discover how much in agreement all four Gospel writers are on the place of women on the first Easter morning. They all record that it was to women that Jesus first appears after His death. Women were about their normal task of looking after the corpse, anointing the body for its long time in the grave. People point out that there are discrepancies about the number of women who were at the tomb. Luke describes several women, those who had been with Him from Galilee, and he names three of them. Mark also names three, although one of the names is different, Salome rather than Joanna. Matthew just mentions two, the same two that both the others named. John concentrates just on one. And yet this does not amount to a contradiction. For the one woman named by all the Gospel writers is Mary Magdalene. Luke has probably the most inclusive account, recalling all the women who were present, whereas each of the others focuses on just a few. And in telling the resurrection event just through the eyes of one woman, Mary Magdalene, John gives us an important detail which deepens our understanding.

Women in John's Gospel

The Gospel of John is different from the synoptics (Matthew, Mark and John, which present a common story of Jesus) in so many other places. We would expect his stories of women to be different too. For John wrote his Gospel not only as a historical narrative, but as an apologetic, as a long argument about who Jesus really is. It is both a chronological eye witness account, but also an interpretation of Jesus's life. John himself explains his motivation for us: "This is the disciple who testifies to these things and who wrote them down. We know that his testimony is true" (John 21:24). In other words, this is a faithful account. But he tells us he never intended to write a comprehensive biography of Jesus, for "many other things" were done and said by Jesus in the presence of His disciples (John 20:30) and they have not been recorded here. John has made a special selection from all that Jesus did. And he tells us clearly, "these are written that you may believe that Jesus is the Christ, the Son of God, and that by believing you may have life in his name" (v.31).

And so it should not surprise us that when we turn to look at the women in John's Gospel we find new insights, and good reasons for believing in Jesus. Some of the women are already well-known and have names: Mary, his mother, his dear friends Mary and Martha, his faithful follower, Mary Magdalene. Some have not appeared before, and they are not named but described: the Samaritan woman at the well, the woman taken in adultery. These two women are not there in any of the synoptics, yet John devotes a good deal of space to recording the incidents about them. What is more, much of the space is given to details about conversations.

The woman taken in adultery is part of the story about Jesus' confrontation with the Pharisees and teachers of the Law (John 8). They know their Law backwards, that Moses commands them in the Law to stone adulterous women. But Jesus does not contend with them about the Law; they would like a legal dispute where they could parade all their knowledge. Instead He gets to the heart of what the law is about: not just scapegoating the sinner, but about confronting one's own sin. His invitation to those without sin to throw the first stone leaves the woman standing alone, where not even Christ condemns her, but asks her to leave her life of sin. The Samaritan woman is, like the adulterous woman, an "outsider" (John 4). She is both a Samaritan, and a woman who has had five husbands and is currently cohabiting. Yet she has a conversation with Jesus that is profound and eternally significant.

If these new women were not remarkable enough, John's stories about the familiar women are also striking in that they are different from the incidents Luke records. Only John tells us about the wedding party at Cana in Galilee where Mary and Jesus are guests (John 2). But he tells it in graphic detail. The wine runs out and Mary, already aware who Jesus really is, and that He can produce the miracle, instructs the servants to get ready to do whatever He says. And Jesus indeed turns water into wine, yet in so unobtrusive a way that the host gets the credit. There is similar new insight in the relationship of Mary and Martha (John 11). For this time John chooses an occasion that is not about domesticity or anxiety over housework, but a dramatic, electrifying incident where their brother is brought back to life.

So John presents things in a different way from the writers of the synoptic Gospels, and his women are shown in distinct light. But he has already told us the reason why – because he is choosing those incidents which will help us to believe. The women in John are subordinated to the Messianic theme to which John devotes his whole Gospel. The moments with women illustrate Jesus's confrontation with the Jewish authorities, with the self–righteous crowds, with his inclusion of the marginalised and the outsider. They are wrapped up with the reminders of the Messianic expectations of the Old Testament, with the miracles the Messiah will perform, with the claims Jesus makes about Himself. And in two key incidents the women are there to hear Jesus give the dramatic disclosure of who He is. When John takes up the great "I Am" theme of Jesus, twice the declaration is made to women.

There is a history to the statement of "I Am". In Exodus 3 Moses is called by God from the burning bush and given a commission to go to Pharoah and to the Israelites and Moses says to God, "Suppose I go to the Israelites and say to them 'The God of our fathers has sent me to you,' and they ask me, 'What is his name?' Then what shall I tell them?" God said to Moses, "I AM WHO I AM. This is what you are to say to the Israelites: 'I AM has sent me to you'" (vv.13–14).

John uses this same self-designation for Jesus (John 8:58): "'I tell you the truth Jesus answered, 'before Abraham was born, I am.'" That must have brought a gasp from those who heard Him. Jesus was putting Himself on a level with the great "I Am" of God: the One who is there through eternity, who has neither beginning nor end. John puts flesh on the great "I Am", and that flesh is Jesus. "I am the bread of life," says Jesus and feeds the five thousand people on the hillside (John 6). "I am the light of the world" says Jesus (John 8), and heals a man born blind. "I am the good shepherd," says Jesus (John 10) and lays down his life for the sheep. "I am the resurrection and the life" says Jesus (John 11), and brings back Lazarus from the dead. "I am the way, the truth and the life," says Jesus (John 14), and draws people to the Father. The great "I ams" are Messianic signs. John does not leave us second guessing. He brings them out to show us the truth about Jesus.

That is why the stories of the conversations Jesus has with women are so important. With both the Samaritan woman, and Martha, John uses the conversation to disclose who Jesus is. He spends time sketching in for us the background to the conversations. In the first one we are in the hottest part of the day. Jesus is thirsty, baking in the heat by the well of Sychar, waiting for the return of His disciples. When a woman comes with a drinking vessel He is not too proud to ask for a drink, and in the conversation that follows the woman recognizes He is a prophet. He tells her about herself, things that no stranger could know. So she has a dozen questions about worship and in a sudden moment of hope she tentatively suggests that when the Messiah comes He will explain all these things. Then comes the extraordinary response. "I am he," says Jesus, "the one who is speaking to you." John does not hide the fact that this is an amazing moment. This woman, who is so little in the world's eyes, has been privileged to receive the self-revelation of the Messiah. John finishes the story off by relating the surprise of the disciples at finding them together, and by letting us know that she becomes the first evangelist.

In Martha's story John again brings out both the disclosure and response. She is grief-stricken that Jesus has not rushed to their help and stopped her brother Lazarus from dying. But even in her misery she still says she believes that her brother will rise again at the resurrection. And then comes another heart-stopping disclosure. Jesus identifies Himself as the resurrection and the life. He asks her if she believes that. Martha's response is so similar to the Samaritan woman's. She makes unashamed testimony to her faith: "Yes, Lord, I believe that you are the Christ, the Son of God, who was to come into the world" (John 11:27).

John does not leave us only with conversations. He follows them with accounts of miracles so amazing that they can only have one explanation; that Jesus is indeed the Messiah of God, the One of whom the prophets have foretold, and for whom the people waited. Both John and the women in his Gospel are utterly convinced. And their stories are told for us to believe.

So whether their stories are told through the eyes of Matthew, Mark, Luke the caring physician, or through John the great evangelist, women are crucially important in the Gospel accounts. Their stories are very specific and particular: narratives of real women who lived and loved and had needs of their own. But their stories are also universal. They speak into the souls of women wherever they are told faithfully and with prayer.

Let us take our cue from the Gospel writers and do our story-telling, from the Bible and our own lives. And let us pray that women who do not yet believe will be drawn into the love and grace of the God who has given us a wonderful story to tell.

Alive for God is a series of faith-building events drawing women together for celebration and encouragement.

Launched in 1998 by *Woman Alive* magazine and Crusade for World Revival, its immediate success indicated a heartfelt need amongst Christian women to worship and learn together.

Combining lively worship with practical teaching, it endeavours to focus on women as women before God, rather than the roles they might fulfil.

All the writers in *Encouraging Women* have spoken at some stage during the tour.

1999 dates are as follows:

BIRMINGHAM	19 June
BRISTOL	3 July
MANCHESTER	2 October
BELFAST	30 October
GLASGOW	20 November

Two speakers at each event. For ticket information on these or future events contact:

CWR, Waverley Abbey House, Waverley Lane,
Farnham, Surrey GU9 8EP
Tel: 01252 784712 Fax: 01252 784722

WOMAN
alive
for today's Christian woman

Woman Alive is the only UK magazine specifically written for today's Christian woman. Its unique editorial blend provides you with the help and encouragement you need. Month by month you will find:

- Real-life testimonies
- Emotional/relationship issues
  – helping you grow through your experiences
- Celebrity profiles and personality interviews
- Spiritual topics, guidelines and Bible readings for building your faith
- Faith in the workplace – at home and at work
- Health and 'green' issues
  – caring for yourself and your neighbour

"*Woman Alive* is ideal – challenging, informing, comforting and relaxing" – Catherine, Worcester.

For a free trial copy phone our subscription hotline: 01903 602100 and quote *Encouraging Women* offer.

OR write to: *Woman Alive*
                 Freepost SEA 2747
                 96 Dominion Road
                 WORTHING
                 West Sussex BN14 8BR

Let CWR unlock the Bible's riches for you!

Day and Residential Courses

Ministry to Women

Books and Devotionals

Counselling Training

Located near Farnham in Surrey, in beautiful Waverley Abbey House, CWR have been involved in publish-ing and training for close on 35 years. Our daily devotional, *Every Day with Jesus*, is read by more than half-a-million people around the world, and our courses in Biblical studies and pastoral care and coun-selling are renowned for their excellence and spiritual impact. To find out more, phone the number below, write to us, or visit our web site – htttp://www.cwr.org.uk.

Biblical Studies Courses

Seminar Videos

Regional Seminars

Audio Cassettes

For your free catalogue of CWR products or a brochure about our seminars and courses, please phone Jo Heather on 01252 784710 or write to: CWR, Waverley Abbey House, Waverley Lane, Farnham, Surrey GU9 8EP.

CWR
CRUSADE FOR WORLD REVIVAL

Applying God's Word to *everyday life and relationships*